Voices from the Classroom

Voices from the Classroom

Elementary Teachers' Experience with Argument–Based Inquiry

Edited by

Brian Hand
University of Iowa

Lori Norton-Meier
University of Louisville

SENSE PUBLISHERS
ROTTERDAM/BOSTON/TAIPEI

A C.I.P. record for this book is available from the Library of Congress.

ISBN: 978-94-6091-449-2 (paperback)
ISBN: 978-94-6091-450-8 (hardback)
ISBN: 978-94-6091-451-5 (e-book)

Published by: Sense Publishers,
P.O. Box 21858,
3001 AW Rotterdam,
The Netherlands
www.sensepublishers.com

Printed on acid-free paper

DEDICATION

To all the teachers who are willing to "have a go" with the SWH Approach and to truly examine daily what it means to teach in the service of learning.

TABLE OF CONTENTS

BRIAN HAND AND LORI NORTON-MEIER

ACKNOWLEDGEMENTS

We have written this book with guidance from a group of teachers, pre-service educators, and professional development providers who have taken on the role of helping teachers learn to use the SWH approach. Many of them have experience in using the SWH approach with students in K-12 classrooms and all have experience at supporting teachers through change. They have provided insight and critical comment making sure that we as authors are focusing on the teachers, their classrooms, and their students. We thank this group. Others have supported the development of our own questions, claims, and evidence:

QUESTIONS

We began with the question, "How can we support teachers to engage students in science and literacy with the SWH approach remembering that we must teach in the service of learning?" To answer this question, we had the help of many school districts, teachers, students, and administrators who joined us in this inquiry, asked their own questions about science and literacy and pushed us every day to think deeply about teaching and learning. This work would not have been possible without the support of a Math-Science Partnership grant and the State of Iowa who supported the teachers and researchers to engage in this investigation.

CLAIMS

Our claim is that this book would not be possible without the support of our colleagues at The University of Iowa, Iowa State University, and The University of Louisville. Specifically we must thank, Tracie Miller, Denise Dadisman, Mitch Williams and Allison Donaldson. Your attention to detail, pep talks, humour, and ability to multi-task made this book an intriguing endeavour. You reminded us daily of the important work we were doing. Daily, this work is made richer through our work with both graduate and undergraduate students who join us in this research endeavour. Also, a special thank you to Sense Publishers and Michel Lokhorst for seeing the value in this project.

EVIDENCE

Once the evidence was gathered, we reflected upon our understanding by writing. The results were overwhelming—when teachers are willing to re-examine their beliefs about teaching and learning and give the process a go, students and teachers are successful. Here we must thank the authors of the chapters of this book who "had a go" with the SWH approach in their own classrooms and took the time to write about their own learning and thinking at this time. The creation of this volume was supported by a Teacher Professional Continuum grant (No. ESI – 0537035) through the National Science Foundation. A consulting group provided extensive feedback on our efforts and pushed our thinking. That group included Lynn Hogue, Mickey Sarquis, John Tillotson, Leah McDowell, Bill Crandall, Kim Wise, and Jodi Bintz. Additionally, an advisory board has also provided thoughtful response and feedback on our efforts including Donna Alvermann, Sharon Dowd-Jasa, Todd Goodson, Kathy McKee, Wendy Saul, and Larry Yore. We thank you for your wisdom and continued "nudging" as we grow in our own understanding of teaching and learning, science and literacy.

And, with extreme gratitude and pride, we thank our families who create spaces and time for us to practice what we teach and continually encourage us to have a go with our many questions, ideas, and projects about teaching and learning.

The development of this volume was supported by the National Science Foundation under grant number ESI–0537035. Any opinions, findings, conclusions or recommendations expressed are those of the authors and do not necessarily reflect the views of the National Science Foundation.

BRIAN HAND AND LORI NORTON-MEIER

INTRODUCTION

Teaching in the Service of Learning

Okay. I am officially hooked. Three of my classes got into arguments about whether or not matter can be created/destroyed or if it just changes. They talked about how energy has to be involved, whether or not a baby is created, what happens to dead animals when they decay, it was awesome! There were excellent points on both sides. I had to put my hand over my mouth to keep from joining them.

I am seeing roughly the same amount of fact retention at this time with SWH as I did when I was teaching with a more traditional lecture/notes method but my kids then would have never been able to argue with evidence as my kids did today. All of this and I have only begun to learn how to teach using SWH, I can't wait until I am halfway skilled in the approach! Thank you for helping us with this, both of you. (Email communication from James Haver, October 15, 2010)

James Haver is a sixth grade teacher who is new to the SWH approach and is in his first year of implementation. In this volume, you will hear the voices of teachers just like James who will share their own professional narratives … narratives that detail their professional journey to implement argument-based inquiry into their own classrooms. Their stories of not only teacher learning but also student learning are compelling. So, just what is this approach that has a group of teachers talking, as James does in his email communication above, about the transformation they see happening in their various classrooms?

There is currently much interest within the science education community on the use of argument-based inquiry approaches within school classrooms. The intent of these approaches are to provide students experiences that are more closely aligned to how science is done, rather than on the traditional inquiry approaches that have been used over the last 10–15 years. There are a number of different perspectives about these approaches ranging from teaching students how to argue before they "do" science argument to teaching science argument as a critical component of an inquiry approach. The editors are firmly in the camp of the latter perspective in that we believe students learn about argument by "living" the argument as part of their inquiries.

This book is intended to provide the opportunity for teachers, who are interested in implementing argument-based inquiry into their classrooms, a chance to look inside the classrooms of teachers who are using the approach. The book brings together teachers from Kindergarten through to grade 6 who have taken a chance on re-thinking about how they teach and have shifted their focus to be about learning rather on themselves as teachers, as well as some of the professional developers who are working with these teachers. All the teacher authors believe that their students need to focus on framing questions, making claims and supporting their claims with evidence. They are firmly committed to the idea that students need to live the language of science by using the language science as they experience it.

ARGUMENT-BASED INQUIRY AND WHAT IS NEEDED

In building a picture of argument-based inquiry, we need to discuss what are the critical elements of argument and how this varies from some of the early inquiry approaches. While there has been much discussion within the science education research community about what are the critical elements of science argument, the translation into practical teaching approaches has not always been clear. Importantly there are a number of different perspectives that researchers have taken in working with teachers. Some approaches highlight the need for students to be involved in critical discourse about science. That is, students need to learn about the importance of how scientists build knowledge. Students need to be able to engage in the argu-mentation approaches that scientists used to advance knowledge. To teach students about this, these approaches advocate a need for students to be taught about argu-ment before they get to use the process. Students need to understand what the argument is, prior to them being engaged in doing science.

While we do not disagree with the idea of students needing to engage with argumentation, we believe that it is necessary for them to be actively involved in building their arguments as a process of learning about argument. We can teach students to engage in inquiry activities based on a questions, claims and evidence structure, that is, an argument-based inquiry approach. Students are full of questions about topics – we just need to let them express them and negotiate which of them are worth exploring. By placing demands on them to negotiate between the data they collect, and what claim they can make from the data, we can push them to deal with the concept of evidence. Children can be pushed to write a narrative that explains what data points they want to use and why they want to use them. We can help them understand that data plus reasoning results in evidence. Evidence is not free of reasoning. This is critical for us because we have to stop students from reporting under evidence or results – "see data" as though data speaks.

The approach used by the teachers in this project is the Science Writing Heuristic (SWH) approach. This approach was developed in the late 1990's by Brian Hand and Carolyn Keys and is intended to encourage students' negotiation of science through an argument-based structure. The following template (heuristic – a problem solving device) is the one a student is required to use for any inquiry activity (See Figure I.1).

As part of using such a structure, students are required to both publicly and privately negotiate what are their claims and evidence. They are constantly required to reason through their data, other students' data and the public debates that are the norm of the classroom environment.

1. Beginning ideas - What are my questions? 2. Tests - What did I do? 3. Observations - What did I see? 4. Claims - What can I claim? 5. Evidence - How do I know? Why am I making these claims? 6. Reading - How do my ideas compare with other ideas? 7. Reflection - How have my ideas changed?

Figure I.1. The SWH approach student template.

The use of such a structure is based around involving students all along the way – they help pose questions, take part in public debate of their claims and evidence, and search the literature to see how their ideas compare with others including the practicing scientists. Science becomes something that they construct and critique, where their ideas are valued and debated, and where words such as "prove" are no longer the norm but replaced by "scientifically acceptable". Science knowledge is to be contested and understood for that knowledge as being the best fit at the current moment.

DO TEACHERS NEED TO CHANGE?

If we want to have children actively involved in a question, claims and evidence approach to inquiry, we are going to have to make changes both in how we think about learning and how we act within the classroom. Rather than trying to talk about it from an academic point of view, we have inserted the words of Josh, one of the teacher authors of this book. He was asked by his school's curriculum coordinator to explain what the SWH approach is all about. He chose to reply in the form of the SWH template.

Claim: The Science Writing Heuristic focuses on student learning. Evidence: Traditionally, teachers are the center of the classroom and all information comes from them. This model of teaching has little impact on the students, in particular critical thinking. The students learn how to play the "guess what's in my head" game, and therefore, can answer the teacher's questions the way he/she wants. This simple recall of information does not cause the students to think critically about what is going on in the classroom.

The following question is essential to understand: What is teaching, and what is learning? When looking at the first part, teaching, one must understand that a teacher can NOT put information into a student's head. The teacher has absolutely zero control of learning. For example, as you are reading this claim and evidence, I cannot "teach" you about teaching and learning. For if I could, you would then agree with me and the conversation would be finished. Rather, you are negotiating what you believe to be true based on your previous negotiations (readings, experiences). So what is teaching? Teaching is the management of the classroom. This is a crucial part of the student's day. As the teacher's management keeps the environment safe and productive, it provides opportunities for the students to negotiate their current understandings.

Learning, the second part of the question is also known as negotiating your previous framework to make new meaning. The complexity of learning comes in when we begin to look at how the teacher's role is so powerful. Even though a teacher has zero control over the learning, they still have 100% control over the environment. Students who are not given public opportunities to negotiate only have private negotiation. Ideas that never go public can't be understood by the teacher (for planning) and cannot be challenged by other students/peers/teacher. If learning is negotiation, what is the level of learning in classrooms without public negotiations?

The focus of SWH is negotiation. In this approach, teachers use the students' interest to gain questions. These questions surrounding the "big idea" then give direction for the class. As the students begin to investigate their questions they begin to find additional support, changes needed, or new ideas about why things are and how they work. All of this is done on various levels: self, peer, expert. Each is equally beneficial.

One might say that SWH is limited to the science classroom. If you step back to look at science, science is language around science. Science is a world of theories that we are continually adjusting by the use of language. If you pulled the language (reading, writing, speaking, listening, symbol/picture, body language) out of the science classroom, you wouldn't be productive. The same would be true for all other subject matter. SWH, rather, is an argument-based approach that makes the curricula both rigorous and relevant. This is not a strategy.

If one truly believes that learning is negotiation, then what does the planning look like? The teacher still decides the "big idea" based on the Iowa Core Curriculum (ICC) and the district's requirements. From that point, the teacher has to look at a concept map of what they know, what is the structure of knowledge for understanding the "big idea", and additional research that may need to be done to understand the topic. Once the structure of the "big idea" is understood by the teacher, then they can start looking for the activities/experiences that could be offered to the classroom when the questions arise. It is critical to start with where the students are with their understanding of the "big idea". A quick pre-activity will allow the teacher

> to know what they do or do not know. This also leads the students into questions. These questions are what would drive the rest of the unit. Activities/experiences are NOT sequential. Rather they should be utilized to best help with parts of the concept map, student questions, and tie back to the ICC.
>
> Traditionally a teacher has set lesson plans from day 1 to day X based on the ICC or district requirements. This past year we looked at rigor and relevance, which I called a strategy for planning. Teachers tried to say why things are relevant. Who are we to say why things are relevant? Is it our learning or the students? Very similarly we tried to develop a unit plan or lesson plan that was rigorous. If we are about the student's learning, why are we planning how an activity will go, what will be done a head of time, and never negotiate?

There are many things being addressed by Josh – the need for negotiation, the setting of, and focus on, the "big ideas" rather than content facts, planning that builds off where the children are, and the idea of a possible non sequential order to the unit. While this list is not exhaustive, it does highlight that there are some significant changes that teachers need to engage with. All of us using this argument-based approach believe that our job is not about teaching but rather about learning. We in science education, and in education in general, have real trouble translating the learning theories that underpin the philosophy of science teaching into classroom practice.

Our focus in working with the teachers is not on a particular curriculum product, or a curriculum that we have developed (we have not done this or are interested in this task), but rather on challenging them to translate learning theory into practice. Every teacher adopts a curriculum to suit him/herself. If we focus on learning theory, and build teaching practices that address the theory, then teachers can use these regardless of what curriculum they asked to use. The SWH approach to argument requires teachers to understand and adopt a learning is negotiation approach to their classroom. While this is difficult, the rewards are significant.

THIS BOOK

Each of the authors or teams of authors have used the SWH approach within their classrooms or in helping teachers to use this approach. The authors have had success with this argument-based inquiry approach. However, the journey has not been easy for them. All the authors have had at least three years experience using the approach. They have all stumbled, been supported through their struggles and are still using the approach.

The chapters are intended to provide you with a snapshot of various aspects of what goes on in their classrooms, or with the professional providers who work with the teachers. The book is intended to help the reader to see that it is not all a bed of roses – it is not going to happen overnight, nor will it be without trouble spots. However, we believe that persistence will be reward.

The authors span teachers of young children through to 5th and 6th grade teachers. The early grade teachers do involve their students in public negotiation – students can make claims and provide evidence for their claims. The older children do develop more sophisticated arguments, but they are still based around a question, claims, and evidence structure. We encourage the reader to read this book in conjunction with our *Question, Claims and Evidence* (QCE) book (Norton-Meier, Hand, Hockenberry & Wise, 2008), as this will help provide the teacher stories behind the how to do the SWH approach which is the focus of the QCE book.

In particular, the reader will see three themes that emerge in this book. The first four chapters focus on the central theme of the SWH approach: *There is no science without language.* Lynn Hockenberry begins with a discussion of how language is used to learn in SWH classrooms followed by a chapter by Michelle Harris where she illuminates the role of discussion in the negotiation of learning. In Chapter 3, Michelle Griffen talks about the breadth of language demonstrating how reading, writing, listening and thinking are essential to the work of children as scientists. Finally, Amy Higginbotham and Christine Sutherland discuss the role of writing to their young students negotiation of meaning both in science and their developing understanding of how language works.

The second theme that appears throughout the volume but is particularly the focus of the next four chapters is that *negotiation is central to learning.* Kim Wise describes the focus on learning in Chapter 5 and how teachers engaging the SWH approach create classrooms where children learn. Following up on Kim's chapter, Joshua Steenhoek, Jill Parsons, and Kari Pingel discuss in Chapter 6 how the SWH lens has created a powerful space where their sixth grade students can negotiate their understandings about challenging science content. In particular, the authors focus on their use of technology to open up the opportunities for ongoing negotiation both in and out of the school setting. Often, members of the professional community doubt if young children can engage in this form of argument-based inquiry. In Chapter 7, Julie Sander details the learning of her kindergarten students who did in fact learn to use argument through science conversations. Peggy Hansen continues the conversation by highlighting the use of the terms claims and evidence in a fifth grade classroom and how this transformed not only her thinking but also that of her students by turning science learning into a space for negotiation.

The final theme is that *only the learner controls learning so we must organize our classrooms so that all students can engage with the big ideas of science.* In Chapter 9, Carrie Johnson talks about her experiences watching the classroom environment transform as teachers engage in argument-based inquiry. To lend a more detailed picture to the discussion of environment, Cheryl Ryan and Gina Johnson describe their third grade classrooms and in particular focus on how the use of nonfiction literature helped transform students thinking and help students learn science conceptually, not just random content facts. Building on their chapter, Julie Malin describes in Chapter 11 how her first grade students use concept maps to build their understanding of science topics while simultaneously experiencing how language helps us think about what we know and how we know it. Finally in Chapter 12, Sara Nelson describes her unique project where she uses music as a tool for students to summarize their learning with putting together science content learned with lyric writing. The result is an important learning experience where students are asked to transfer what they know into a new context.

We ask you to enjoy this journey that will take you through the pages of this text. As researchers, teachers, professional development providers, administrators, parents, and other interested community members, we believe this book has many lessons to be learned about teacher learning, teacher transformation, and how we support teachers to continually be able to challenge what they know and how we can continue to orchestrate opportunities for all students to learn in our classrooms. We started this introduction with an email message from James who has just started this journey with the SWH approach ... it is our hope that this volume will let him know as well as those of you reading this text also, that many have taken this journey and continue to ask important questions about teaching and learning. Let our journey continue.

REFERENCE

Norton-Meier, L., Hand, B., Hockenberry, L., & Wise, K. (2008). Questions, claims, and evidence: The important place of argument in children's science writing. Portsmouth, NH: Heinemann.

Brian Hand
Science Education
University of Iowa

Lori Norton-Meier
Literacy Education
University of Louisville

LYNN HOCKENBERRY

1. USING LANGUAGE TO LEARN

As a literacy consultant, I have the opportunity to travel to and work with many schools, teachers, and students in K-12 settings. One of the most important aspects of my work is that of supporting the Science Writing Heuristic (SWH) approach to teaching and learning. On a dreary early winter day, my travels took me to one of my favorite schools in a small town in Southwest Iowa. My intention that morning was to quickly touch base with the fifth grade teacher and establish a time for a future observation. The teacher met me at the door with a smile and said, "Do you have a minute? I would love for you to see the writing my students are doing!" At that point, I sensed the dreary day would soon be forgotten and this would definitely not be a "quick stop."

I listened as the teacher began describing a recent day in Science. Students were at the point in their SWH investigation where they were reading to explore "what do others say". She told me that she decided to try something new and have students investigate the ways in which authors of non-fiction structure and organize text. Students generated charts (See Figure 1-1) noting what authors of non-fiction did to help their readers understand the science content. The teacher spoke excitedly as she described the enthusiasm students had for this task. After exploring non-fiction text and creating charts, her students asked if they could write their journal entries in a similar manner. Because she understands the power of students using language to learn her response was an immediate, "Of course". She was excited and amazed at the ways in which students were now demonstrating their understanding in their science journals.

As she finished explaining this process to me, she asked students if they wanted to share their writing with me. The response of the students was an overwhelming, "Yes". All of the students reached into their desks, pulled out their journals and turned to their most recent entries. They all wanted to show me their "non-fiction" writing. Smiling, I walked from one group of students to the other, reading each and every non-fiction entry. Each student provided me a detailed explanation of the reasons they chose to write their entry in this manner.

Here are sample conversations from three different students that morning. A confident young man told me, "I had different words that were bolded and wrote what they meant, "transparent", "translucent" and "opaque" and then (I drew) a picture to go with them. I wrote what happens to a white light when it goes through a prism and drew this picture" (See Figure 1-2).

When his teacher asked him to tell me what he liked about writing in this way, he said, "I personally think it is a much better way to record my thinking because I can understand it in a better way. I remember it better because of the picture."

B. Hand and L. Norton-Meier, (eds.), Voices from the Classroom: Elementary Teachers'
Experience with Argument–Based Inquiry, 1–12.

Figure 1-1. Students generated charts noting what authors of non-fiction did to help their readers understand the science content.

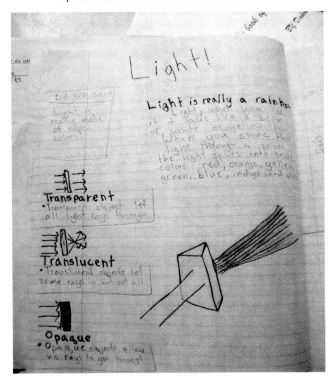

Figure 1-2. A student writing sample where he uses text features to demonstrate his understanding.

Another young man in the group said, "Sometimes when I read text and see a word I don't know, usually if it has a picture; I can understand it better, so I wrote this way." He turned his journal toward me so I could read and see the picture he had drawn to explain the word "opaque".

I walked toward another group of students sitting at a cluster containing three desks. Shyly, a young lady handed me her journal. She said "I wrote words over here and then drew pictures of what it (each word) is for and then I wrote, "The sound is traveling through the wall".

As you might imagine from my description, my "quick stop" became an hour conversation with students. What a day brightener! I was so happy to have the opportunity to read, listen, talk, view and share the excitement of learning with these young scientists and authors. As is often the case after observing and conversing with students and teachers in SWH classrooms, I was excited and delighted to see and hear the learning that was occurring inside these four walls. Students were engaging in science content **and** they were using language to negotiate their own understanding and communicate that understanding to themselves and others.

Before I became a literacy consultant, I implemented the SWH approach in my classroom for several years. The very thing I loved as a classroom teacher, watching children discover the joy and excitement of learning, was clearly evident in this classroom. This morning's visit was a reminder and a testament to the power of using language to learn and the SWH approach.

THERE IS NO SCIENCE WITHOUT LANGUAGE

The SWH approach holds as a central belief "There is no Science without language" (Norton-Meier, Hand, Hockenberry, Wise, 2008). Language (writing, reading, speaking, listening, and viewing) is fundamental to this approach. A cornerstone then to the approach is that we "use language to learn" (Norton, Meier, Hand, Hockenberry, Wise, 2008). In the classroom described above, students had investigated the ways in which authors of non-fiction science text structured and communicated their ideas. Their investigation led them to discover that most non-fiction texts have certain text features; bold print, colored font, headings, captions, labels, pictures-photographs or drawings, boxes containing key ideas or information, glossaries, etc. Students were then given the opportunity to write in their journals in "a non-fiction way". As their journal writing and verbal reflection indicates these students are using language by reading, writing, viewing, and speaking as apprentices in the disciplines of **both** science and language. In this case, I refer to the definition of an apprentice as "a learner" or "one who is learning a trade or occupation" (Dictionary.com, 2010).

If we think about these students as apprentices, then why is it beneficial to apprentice students in the use of **both** language and science? According to Carolyn Shanahan (2004, p. 75), a lab scientist was asked "how much time he spent in reading and writing activities associated with his job. He said that he read and wrote approximately 99% of the time he was at work." In addition, Shanahan states "Reading and writing about science is also required of anyone who wishes to be an informed consumer or an engaged citizen". In this same chapter, Shanahan (2004, p. 89) discusses results of a study by Tucknott and Yore (1999) in which they found that "4th graders improved their understanding of simple machines when they learned how to take notes, make summaries, and write sentence and paragraph explanations for drawings and labels." Studying the writing of non-fiction authors leads to authentic representation of the work of scientists who use "labels, graphs, equations, tables, diagrams, and models" (Hand, 2008) as well as written text to communicate their ideas. The students in this 5th grade classroom are well on their way to becoming "real" scientists.

EXAMPLES OF WAYS IN WHICH STUDENTS USE LANGUAGE (WRITING)
TO LEARN THROUGHOUT THE SWH APPROACH

Writing in a "non-fiction way" is just one way that students in SWH classrooms use language to learn. The students in the 5th grade classroom I have been describing agreed to share with us some other ways in which they use writing to learn about science concepts. As is customary at the beginning of an SWH unit the teacher, in order to identify students' current understanding and plan for instruction, had students create a concept map. Using a concept map helps teachers identify students' current understanding and make plans for instruction. A concept map centers around what student know and understand about the big idea of a science unit. The big idea is a kid friendly conceptual statement, which aligns to the science essential concept. Development of a concept map helps students orient themselves to the big idea while drawing upon their past experiences and connecting with what they currently understand related to the science concept.

As Hillocks (1987, p. 72) states "Children need to learn to conduct a memory search to help them tap into the knowledge that they have about a concept. Students appear to need to do a memory search to gather their thoughts." Concept maps allow students not only to conduct a "memory search" but also to link their understanding in ways that our brain naturally organizes information. Importantly, it provides a visual representation of their thinking, which is key for both students and the teacher. Here is how one-fifth grade student explained the development and importance of a concept map:

A concept map is like where we write down the main deal, which is energy, and what we are learning about energy, which is light, sound and heat. We have different color writing utensils. The pencil is what we learned first, the red pen is what we learned second, and the black pen is what we learned over the whole unit. It is different than a word web because it uses connecting words. We write down what we learned to help us remember.

Thus the concept map becomes not only a tool to help to help both the teacher and the student identify current understanding, but a tool to help students reflect upon and consolidate their learning. When students use language (in this case writing) to learn, it serves as a "catalyst for further learning-an opportunity for students to recall, clarify, and question what they know and what they still wonder about" (Fisher, Frey, & Elwardi, 2004, p. 140). This process is vital to the negotiation of one's own understanding of a concept.

Students also spoke about the use of the SWH student template as a way to record their thinking during science investigations. A 5th grade girl described the use of the template during her recent science investigation regarding sound:

Mostly we write down our beginning idea, which is just what we think. Then we do (write) our procedure-our lab...what we do to "See what happens". Our observations are what we heard or saw. Then we make a claim and write our evidence.

As indicated earlier, the work of scientists is heavily invested in reading and writing. When students use the SWH template they are writing to learn in a focused manner. Using the template allows students to negotiate their understanding individually and/or with their small group before engaging in discussion with peers and sharing their claim and evidence.

ARGUMENTATION AND PUBLIC NEGOTIATION AS LANGUAGE TOOLS FOR LEARNING

During the sharing of claims and evidence, students are engaged in yet another aspect of using language to learn, that of argumentation and public negotiation of understanding. While discussing claims and evidence in this classroom, the teacher is particularly mindful of students who may be negotiating their understanding privately, but are not sharing their thinking aloud with other students. She uses "Pause and Reflect" as an opportunity for students to stop talking and record their thoughts. By using "Pause and Reflect" the teacher invites students to "compose their thoughts and take stock of their beliefs and opinions before engaging in (further) discussion" (Fisher, Frey, & Elwardi, 2004, p. 151). In the words of a self-described "quiet" 5th grade girl:

Sometime we have a big discussion and some people don't get to talk and then we write down what we are thinking to see if what we thought is what we still think. We use it so we can understand what we are thinking. If you are a really quiet person and you can't talk because everyone is talking, you get to write it down. Sometimes I don't talk, but I pause and reflect to think about my ideas.

This student showed me two pages of writing she had composed during "Pause and Reflect". It was an amazing explanation of her thinking! Without this opportunity to write, both she and her teacher would not have known the depth of her understanding related to the concept. Even though she chose not to publicly negotiate her understanding by speaking, her writing could lead to a public negotiation in the form of summary writing at the end of the unit.

SUMMARY WRITING

Thus far, we have been exploring the ways in which students use language to learn for the purpose of negotiating their own understanding and with the primary audience being themselves. The writing format varied from "writing in a non-fiction way" to "using the SWH template for labs" to jotting down ideas from "Pause and Reflect" to the use of the concept map.

Another key piece of using language to learn within the SWH approach is for students to engage in summary writing to an audience other than themselves or their

5

teacher. The reading and writing that students engage in throughout the SWH process becomes the catalyst for this summary writing experience. Let us think back to the beginning of this chapter. Students were writing "in a non-fiction way" in their notebooks. Students made the connection between reading and writing and demonstrated this in their "new" way of writing. This writing then can be used and expanded on in summary writing. It is the act of summary writing (particularly to a younger audience) that consolidates students' thinking around the big idea. Examples of summary writing include, but are not limited to: writing letters, creating books, making field guides, brochures, and writing poems. For a more complete list of ideas for summary writing, please see Chapter 8 of *Questions, Claims, and Evidence* (2008), by Norton Meier, Hand, Hockenberry, and Wise.

Not long after visiting the classroom described above, I had the opportunity to talk to students in another 5th grade classroom about their summary writing. These students had just completed a unit centered on the human body. As a part of this unit, they had completed multiple investigations and read many, many non-fiction books to find out "what others say". They too had compiled information about what non-fiction writers did to help their audience understand their message. They were particularly intrigued by "ABC" books and decided to write their own Human Body ABC books for summary writing (See Figure 1-3).

Here is how one young lady described what she learned while she was writing her ABC book:

> I didn't know how I was going to find words for each letter of the book to describe the human body till I started looking things up. For example, I learned a new word, "zooist". Also, our big idea is that Systems work together, and. And they work together very fast. Like your mind...when you have your hand over the stove, it's very hot. Your brain sends a signal to your hand to move through the nerves and right back. It's very fast, lightning fast-very cool. I do love science.

She went on to talk to me about every page in her book at rapid fire pace. She was very proud of her writing and was excited to have the opportunity to talk about her book. What was exciting to me as I listened to her was not only what she had

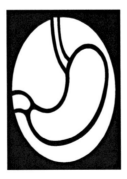

Figure 1-3. Gastric juices break down the food you just ate.

internalized about the human body, but the excitement she had about writing, science, and her learning! Writing was not a "chore" or "just another thing" she had to do for school. She used language to learn and became an author in the process!

USING LANGUAGE TO LEARN IN PRIMARY GRADES

You may be thinking right now, "Ok this is all well and good for upper elementary students, but what about younger students. How do they use language to learn?" Answering this question causes me to smile. My journey first as a teacher and then as a literacy consultant has taken me along many paths and through many different grade levels. In addition to teaching students in upper elementary as I mentioned earlier in this chapter, I spent three years teaching preschoolers with disabilities and one year each teaching students in kindergarten and first grade. Young children are constantly using language to learn. They negotiate their understanding by speaking. They ask questions constantly. They say "You know what", and happily explain to you and to anyone who listens their new understanding of the world. They listen to books and to explanations from their friends, their teachers and their parents, and add to their understanding. They write and draw to make sense of their world. As they write, they are consolidating their understanding of the world while using language to learn. To illustrate this, let's visit a kindergarten classroom.

In this particular visit, which took place in a two hour time period, I had the opportunity to witness what I would call an "explosion" of students using language as a tool for learning. In this kindergarten classroom the teacher had just started a unit centered on the big idea that "Living things have characteristics that make them different from non-living things". She and her class had listed on a large white board items that fit their current understanding of "living things" and "non-living things". Looking around the room, I could see that she had many, many books in her classroom for students to use to consult the experts and she told me that she had encouraged students to read and then write what they had learned. While students were working, the teacher began conferring with individual students to ascertain their beginning understanding about the big idea. She called each student to a quiet spot in the room and asked questions. The conversations went something like this...

Teacher, "Let's talk about living and non-living things. What's your claim about a tree?"

Student, "it's living."

Teacher, "What's your evidence that a tree is alive?"

Student, "It grows."

Teacher, "What's your claim about a chair?"

Student, "Non-living."

Teacher, "What's your evidence?"

To this the student did not respond and simply shrugged his shoulders. The teacher probed further and it became clear that the student was not sure why the chair was non-living. He looked at the teacher's chair and at the other chairs in the room. Skillfully, the teacher probed, "What do you think?" Together they talked more about the chair and determined it couldn't move by itself, so it must not be living.

Each student she interviewed had varied responses. Students were very early in their investigation and were still negotiating their understanding as evidenced by their responses to her.

As I listened to the interviews I glanced around the room and saw that the students who had been reading books were beginning to write on the large white board. I went over and talked to a young lady who was busily writing (See Figure 1-4) and said, "Tell me what you wrote..."

She said, "Raccoons are living. Birds are living and rabbits are living."

I probed further asking, "How do you know?"

She responded, "I know raccoons are living because sometimes when my mom is driving I see raccoons on the road. They move with little feet. Birds are living because they have special parts to move like wings and feet. Rabbits have parts to move with their back legs. I saw some at my house when my brother was shooting birds."

Intrigued by the ways in which she was writing to learn as well as talking about her learning, I smiled at her and sat down with my computer on my lap to listen and engage in one of my favorite activities "kid watching". Students began coming up to me and showing me their books. "Look at this kitten. It's alive... I have a kitten...Do you have a kitten?" said one little girl. One of her classmates who wanted his turn to talk to me said, "Cats are alive, cause I had a cat in my backyard by my dad's old truck. We have cats that don't die."

Figure 1-4. A young child writes her claim on a white board.

As I continued to watch and listen I noticed that several children were picking up small white boards and writing what they were thinking and learning. A young girl sat down by me and drew three columns on her white board. The columns said, "Living, Non Living and?" Puzzled I asked, "What's the question mark for?" She said, "Well, if you don't know if something is living or not, you put it in the question mark spot." Then she began writing. (See Figure 1-5). She said, "A person is alive cause it can move. A car or truck is not alive cause it can't move by itself. A Barbie I don't know. It could be alive and maybe it isn't alive. I just don't know."

These types of conversations continued for the half hour I was able to stay in this room. I looked up at the large white board as I stood to leave and realized that many students had been writing their claims about items that were living and non-living and some were even beginning to write evidence statements. One group of two children wrote, "Cows are living clos (cause) they eat." Reluctantly, I left the classroom and went to my next appointment. An hour later, the kindergarten teacher stopped me outside her room and said, "You have to come see what has happened." Her entire white board was filled with writing!

It was truly an explosion of using language to learn about science. Students were reading, asking questions, sharing claims and evidence with their teacher, with me, and with their classmates. They were writing, thinking, reading, and writing more. All of this occurred because the teacher purposefully set up an environment in which students were in control of their learning and could negotiate their understanding by using language to learn about their world and their big idea.

Figure 1-5. A young student uses writing to organize her thinking.

CONNECTIONS ACROSS GRADE LEVELS

Think back to the examples from 5th grade at the beginning of this chapter. What are the connections between the two in terms of using language to learn? In both cases, students were exploring their understanding by using language to learn. In both cases students were reading, writing, speaking, and listening. In both classrooms students engaged in writing in "non-fiction" ways. Kindergarten students were using cause and effect statements. 5th grade students used concept maps to show the connections between their ideas. Kindergarten students drew two and three column charts and worked to complete them. 5th grade students used other features of text such as bold print and illustrations. Kindergarten and 5th grade students read and wrote to gain understanding of the science concept. They had a purpose to read and a purpose to write. In much the same way as the lab scientist Shanahan (2004) described, they were using language to negotiate their understanding of science in purposeful authentic ways!

To understand further how primary students use language to learn I want to share an example of a first grade student who was participating with his classmates in a claims and evidence discussion after an investigation. In March of this year, I observed this young man for the first time. Thomas had large brown inquisitive eyes and an infectious grin. I was invited to participate in the circle conversation held by the students and their teacher. One by one each student shared their claim and stated their evidence for their claim. After each claim, students were asked if they agreed or disagreed with each claim and to explain their thinking. After the first student made her claim, Thomas said while nodding his head up and down, "I disagree". The teacher said, "Can you please tell us why?" Thomas said, "Because my claim is exactly the same." The teacher said, "Oh, you mean you agree." Thomas said, "That's right, I disagree with Shannon" all the while nodding his head up and down vigorously. After each claim, this conversation was repeated until all the students said, "No, no, you mean you agree." Smiling, he said, "That's what I said, I disagree".

Clearly Thomas was just beginning to use the language of negotiation and the terms "agree" and "disagree". After class, the teacher and I discussed Thomas' conversations. We both agreed that Thomas needed time to further negotiate his own understanding of the differences between the two terms "agree and disagree". His classmates tried to help him understand the differences, as did his teacher. Thomas however, had not yet come to understand. He was determined to use his current understanding as he participated in the conversations. As I drove away from the school that day, I carried a bit of Thomas with me. His smile, his determination to use the language that his classmates were using (even though he did not have operational understanding of the words "agree" and "disagree") was a true example of how children use language to learn.

Almost exactly one month later, I had the opportunity to again observe Thomas in his classroom. The students were seated in their conversation circle sharing claims and evidence. I was excited to see what would happen this time. A young man, Sam, shared his claim and evidence first. Immediately, Thomas began to talk.

"I agree with Sam", he said smiling. "Sam is right; cats do have a life cycle. They are born, they grow, and grow and then eventually they die." His teacher looked up at me and we both smiled. We had evidence on which we both could agree. Thomas now understood the difference between the words "agree" and "disagree".

Through the writing of this chapter, I have tried to share with you examples across grade levels of how students use language (reading, writing, speaking, viewing, and listening) to learn. There is no Science without language; of that there is no doubt. When students are given opportunities to negotiate their own understanding of the world around them by using language to learn, they are truly apprentices on a journey to becoming lifelong learners who will become "informed consumers" and "engaged citizens" (Shanahan, 2004).

CHALLENGES AND HOPES FOR THE FUTURE

The challenges for the future are, in my opinion, opportunities more than challenges. Currently teachers around the world are using the SWH approach. The opportunity we have then is to negotiate our mutual understanding so that we can provide even greater growth in students' conceptual understanding. Negotiation around our mutual understandings will be critically important as we continue to share this approach with more and more teachers and their students. Since we believe that students use language to learn, we will need to think about ways that we can provide more opportunities for students to negotiate their understanding by using language. Questions include:
- What additional tools and resources could teachers use?
- How can we better utilize concept maps, the SWH template, reading frames, student notebooks, and non-fiction print to provide opportunities for students to negotiate understanding?
- What skills and strategies do teachers need to facilitate argumentation in their classrooms?
- How can we better help students use language to learn as they participate in argumentation?

As we move forward and share the approach with more teachers, negotiating our understanding about these and other questions will be critical to improving practice.

Certainly, my hope is that every teacher will embrace the philosophies of teaching and learning that are central to the SWH approach. We know from the tremendous amount of data collected and analyzed in SWH grants, that when teachers approach their classrooms as places where students are in charge of their learning, and provide students with daily opportunities to engage in using language to learn, tremendous growth occurs for all students. Those of us who have worked both as teachers and consultants on this project know first-hand the benefits. We see the excitement, the joy of learning, the engagement of students who want to read, write, listen, view and discuss, and we want these experiences for all students. I believe that Thomas would say, "I agree." Do you?

REFERENCES

Dictionary.com Unabridged. Retrieved April 05, 2010, from Dictionary.com website: http://dictionary. reference.com/browse/apprentice

Fisher, D., Frey, N., & ElWardi, R. (2004). The power in the pen: Writing to learn. In D. Fisher & N. Frey, *Improving adolescent literacy: Strategies at work*, (pp. 139–152). Upper Saddle River, NJ: Pearson.

Hand, B. (2008). *Science inquiry, argument and language: A case for the science writing heuristic.* Rotterdam, The Netherlands: Sense Publishers.

Hillocks, G. (1987). Synthesis of research on teaching writing. *Educational Leadership, 44*(8), 71–82.

Norton-Meier, L., Hand, B., Hockenberry, L., & Wise, K. (2008). Questions, claims, and evidence: The important place of argument in children's science writing. Portsmouth, NH: Heinemann.

Shanahan, C. (2004). Teaching science through literacy. In T. L. Jetton & J. A. Dole (Eds.), *Adolescent literacy research and practice*. New York: Guilford Press.

Tucknott, J. M., & Yore, L. D. (1999, March). *The effects of writing activities on Grade 4 children's understandings of simple machines, inventions and inventors.* Paper presented at the National Association for Research in Science Teaching, Boston.

Lynn Hockenberry
Green Hills Area Education Agency
Atlantic, Iowa, USA

MICHELLE HARRIS

2. NEGOTIATION

Why Letting Students Talk is Essential

Come take a walk in my classroom. I have the students' desks in groups. There is a concept map on the whiteboard. The typed list of student-generated questions is posted on the board. A pile of nonfiction books lay on the table. The tall stack of science journals is waiting to be checked.

This was not the way my classroom looked before I learned about a new approach to teaching science called the Science Writing Heuristic (SWH) six years ago. I was the typical science teacher. I was a new teacher that let the textbook drive my instruction. I used worksheets for students to provide answers to questions about what we read. Maybe I used an occasional lab, but it was highly structured and I was looking for everyone to reach the same answer. I was also apprehensive about teaching science.

Before learning and using the SWH approach, I didn't enjoy teaching science. It was probably my least favorite subject to teach. I truly felt I was not smart enough to teach the topics I needed to teach in upper elementary. I wondered if I truly understood the concepts. What if a student asked me a question and I didn't know the answer? I would be horrified! I certainly didn't encourage students to ask me questions for this very reason.

This is not my classroom today! The textbook is only a resource. We seldom, if at all, do worksheets. My labs are not as structured, and I am elated when students reach different claims on a lab. This makes for terrific debate. Questions are now an essential part of the way I teach science. I realize that it is OK not to know the answer. I can learn with my students, which I do, and teach them ways to locate the answers to their questions. These changes in my instruction did not come easy, nor did they all come at once. It took time and a lot of trial and error. I constantly learn with and from my students.

The focus of this chapter is negotiation. What is negotiation? When does it happen? It happens each day in my classroom and not only during science class. It might be students negotiating with themselves inside their head. It might be students negotiating with other students verbally. It might be students negotiating their own understanding through writing.

What is negotiation? Negotiation is trying to make sense of what you know. Combining what you think you know and listening to what someone else is saying and coming out with your interpretation or understanding. It is questioning your

B. Hand and L. Norton-Meier, (eds.), Voices from the Classroom: Elementary Teachers'
Experience with Argument–Based Inquiry, 13–23.

own thinking or the thinking of others. There are several places negotiation happens in my classroom, and each way will be explained.

CONCEPT MAPS

Concept maps are an excellent tool for negotiation. I use both individual and class concept maps. Individual concept maps are good for self-negotiation. Students need to think about what they know about a topic and how it all fits together. I usually have students make an individual map first. This way everyone has time to think about what they know before we move into the class map. It is important to give students this time to self-negotiate before moving to the whole group. This gives students time to think about how the topic or unit connects in their mind.

When the students are constructing the class concept map the discussion can get pretty heated. Some students are sure they know what they are talking about, but others have no idea. Sometimes a word gets thrown around, but no one knows how to connect it to the bigger picture of the unit of study. There are times when the class just can't agree on how a word fits on the map so it ends up in the "don't know" box until it is determined later in the unit.

I learn a lot during these discussions. I learn who has a lot of background knowledge on the subject. I learn which students might need extra support as the unit progresses. I can discover which students might need to dig deeper into the content to find things that are new to them. I find out what misconceptions the students have. I can tell which students have the right words but have no idea what they mean. I hear questions that are brought up. This is not a time for me to sit back, but instead I am making lots of observations and in a way "taking notes" to know what I need to do next and how I will get there.

Students enjoy watching the concept map grow as we progress through the unit. It is a perfect place to show how our ideas change. What they thought they knew at the beginning of the unit sometimes isn't exactly true. At the end of the school year, it was time to erase our class concept map on the human body. This was the first time during my six years that students asked if they could take a picture of it. I said yes, and before I knew it about six students took out their cell phones and started snapping photos. It showed me that they were proud of their learning.

MY STRUGGLES WITH CONCEPT MAPS

I didn't always understand the importance of or even like using concept maps. They took time, and it was a hassle to find a place to hang it. When I used sticky notes they always fell off. I was unsure of how to handle disagreements between students about where to place words on the map or which connection words to use. Sometimes the knowledge is so varied from student to student that it is hard to come to a class consensus and know how to best construct the map. I thought it might be easier to just avoid the issue. Plus I would forget to come back to the class concept map to revise or add. It seemed like just something I was supposed to do rather than a teaching tool. Couldn't I get the same information from a KWL?

But my problem with KWL's is that I seldom remembered to have students fill in the "What I Learned" column at the end of the unit.

My experience with concept maps is different now. Once I started using them on a regular basis, I found they help students. They gave my students a way to connect their ideas and explain what they knew, instead of just random words about a concept or idea, which would be a word web. And once the kids got hooked, it was easy sailing. My students loved watching the concept map grow during the unit! I realized that the individual students would have varied knowledge, but that was positive because it led to stronger debates and more negotiation.

It is hard not to persuade students' thinking during the negotiation of the concept map. It is another example of a time when I just have to be quiet and let the students take charge. It is their thinking and not the teacher's ideas. When my class made a concept map of the human body the word circularity system was mentioned. Every student in the class called it the circularity system. It wasn't easy for me to write or say that word knowing it was incorrect, but because I knew it wasn't my map and had to go with their word. It stayed on the board wrong throughout the unit it was finally discovered by a student that the system was actually the circulatory system. I knew the students would eventually notice it, but I needed them to point it out.

BEGINNING IDEAS

When my students are first given a question for a lab, I have them write down their beginning ideas on what they think the answer is. I didn't do this my first few years, but I found that students need time to think about what they know or what they think the answer to the question might be. I also ask students to reflect on how their ideas have changed, and I found that if they didn't take time to write down their beginning ideas it was hard to reflect on how their ideas changed. I was displeased with a lot of reflections because I knew the response I would get was "My ideas didn't change". Well, for most students I knew that wasn't true. At first I thought it was just a way out of having to write or a way to make it look like they always knew the correct answer. After reflecting on this issue I came to realize that it might be because they truly did forget what they originally thought. I thought it would be beneficial to write down beginning ideas so students could have a reference point. Also, I feel it is a way for students to commit to an idea. It is easy for students to just say, "I don't know."

IT IS OK TO SAY, "I DON'T KNOW"

This is another issue that I have struggled with. Do I let a student write, "I don't know"? At first I said yes they could write that, but after thinking about it, I have changed my mind. Again I don't want them to take the easy way out. I want students to think, but on the other hand I also know we study some topics the student will have little prior knowledge. My point is I want students to think about what they know. It's too easy to say, "I don't know". I want more than that! I feel there is little to no negotiation if I say it is acceptable to write I don't know.

Once students have self-negotiated, they share their ideas in their small group before beginning their lab. Now we are moving into group negotiation. Students talk about their ideas and now have to think about the ideas of their peers. Do I agree with what she is telling me? Do I understand what he is saying? How does what I am hearing fit with my current understanding or knowledge on the topic? This student-to-student conversation is critical in my classroom. For students to be able to share their ideas and learn from other students is far more powerful than when the knowledge comes directly form me.

After students have completed a lab they are asked to look at their data and observations and make a claim to answer the original question. This claim is to be supported with evidence from data and observations. Again negotiation is important in this step of the SWH approach. First students must self-negotiate. What is this data telling me? Can I support that claim with evidence? Students also listen to the ideas of the other group members and ask themselves if they agree or disagree with the idea. Once again communication is the key.

STRUGGLES WITH CLAIMS AND EVIDENCE

Part of my struggle has been with posing the right question. I have an idea of what knowledge I want students to come out with, but I struggle with aligning the question so those ideas will come out right. I also don't want the question too limited that might cause all groups to come to the same claim. That hasn't happened much for me, which is great. What causes much debate is when two groups have contradicting or opposite claims. It is even better when a student points that out!

I have also found that it is hard for students to make claims. This might sound funny because they are always making statements, but when students have to look at the data and make a factual statement I have found this to be difficult for them. Partly because some of the students might already think they have an answer to the question, but it is more of prior knowledge than a claim they can support with evidence from the lab they completed. For example, my class completed a lab on blood types. This is one of those labs where I struggle to post the question correctly. The question I asked was "What can happen when two bloods are mixed?" One boy couldn't agree with his group and decided to write his own claim, but it was his prior knowledge and didn't come from anything his group did in class. He was trying to make a claim about genetics. Well, there was absolutely no evidence from our lab to support his claim. I have found in my six years that the gifted students struggle the most with claims and evidence. They are certain they know the answer, but when asked for evidence they struggle to provide it. Learning has come easy for those who know the answers or were able to memorize everything after hearing or seeing it. The SWH approach to learning asks the student to think critically and not just memorize.

They also confuse claims and evidence. In their science journals, we write the definition of both. A claim is a scientifically based opinion. Evidence is data that supports your claim or answers the original question. It comes from the observations during the lab. I didn't always do this, but have found it beneficial for the students to reference these questions. Many times students referred to that during debates.

Elementary students can really debate ideas. Science debates are the best part of the entire SWH approach, and a time when I have to close my mouth and listen. Believe me that was not easy to do when I first started this approach to teaching science. Actually, it still isn't, but I have witnessed the benefits of staying out of the conversation. This helps remind me to close my mouth! It is not just a time to sit and do nothing, but instead, it is a time of considerable observation and learning for me as the teacher.

REASONS TO LET STUDENTS DEBATE IN THE CLASSROOM

I learn so much from student debates. I can tell which students "get it" and which ones don't. I take note of what misconceptions are lingering in their minds. I can learn where we should go next or what the next lab or activity should be. I want as much student-to-student talk as possible. Watching my student do this is the highlight of my day, and for the last six years, it is also the favorite part for my students. They are given an opportunity to talk. How often do we ask students what they think about a question or idea? How many teachers want to know what their students think? This goes far beyond a simple KWL chart. Student talking is the backbone of the way I teach science.

My students can hold an hour-long debate and sometimes we will only discuss three claims. There are times when I might not say anything for ten minutes and believe me the room isn't quiet either! I enjoy watching students use higher order thinking questions with each other. They address a certain student to ask them a to clarify something said or directly ask them a question. This is when I know that these debates work. When they start to ask other students what do you think, Joey? I'm in awe. I even wonder sometimes if they need me anymore. This is where I want them to be able to hold a debate amongst themselves. Not only in science, but in all subjects and even outside of the classroom.

STUDENT EXAMPLES

Shy Girl Speaks Up

It was neat to see the quiet student confidently tell her classmates I think we are all wrong. I think light bounces off everything otherwise we wouldn't see anything. She was right, and it took her courageous statement against the other claims to change the course of our conversation. The conversation moved from "Only shiny things reflect light" to "Oh, she might be right!" I wanted to scream yes! You go girl! I am proud of you for going against the ideas of the class. It is easy to go with the flow. Students agree to what the majority of the class thinks or the students that are viewed the "smart ones". I could tell she had been listening to the ideas of her peers and self-negotiating. Something just wasn't fitting with what she was hearing, and she voiced that to the class. This made the class self-negotiate. Some students began saying Oh, yah. I remember reading that in a book.

No Conceptual Understanding

Another example happened during a lab on the respiratory system. Students had completed the lab, written claims, and we were in the middle of the debate. Students had made a model of the respiratory system using a water bottle with the bottom cut off, balloons, straws, tape, and clay. Students knew that the bottom balloon was important in making the lungs expand and contract, but they didn't know what that bottom balloon was in the body. Sometimes students think they know a lot about a topic as in this case with the respiratory system. A few of my students could rattle off the words like lungs and diaphragm, but once other students questioned them, it was revealed that it was just surface level knowledge. No conceptual understanding was there at all. They knew there was a diaphragm, but not a one of them connected that to the bottom balloon. Too often students can say the right things so teachers think they understand it, but this case shows they may not. It just took a few questions to find out they didn't know how the respiratory system worked. This supports the idea of why we need to question students.

Connecting to Past Learning

A third example came from a bright student. He offered the idea of a third lung. He said that maybe that bottom balloon in the model of the respiratory system was a third lung. You might imagine there was quite a bit of buzz in my room about that comment, but it again caused students to negotiate. They came to the conclusion that no one had ever heard about our body having three lungs. Someone else commented that maybe it was a muscle. She said, "You know we just learned about muscles and muscles pull. Maybe that bottom balloon is a muscle." WOW! This is a teacher's dream. Someone is connecting previous learning with something new. It wasn't just taught, tested, and forgotten. She had actually learned that. Muscles pull! Another moment when I just wanted to go up to her and give her a big bear hug and scream Yes! I love moments like that. After six years of teaching with the SWH approach, there are more of these moments each year.

Why You Should Question All Answers...Even the Right Ones

I learned the importance of not only questioning wrong answers, but to question right answers too. I was teaching a language lesson on compound words. I wrote a variety of compound words, some as one word, some as two words, and others with hyphens. I asked the class to figure out what the words had in common. Students first thought alone, then were asked to confer with their group members. Once groups had their ideas we shared out. When the idea of compound words came up, I asked a student, "Really, I thought compound words were just two words put together to form one word?" She instantly doubted her answer and said that now she didn't know. No one else now wanted to say they were all compound words. I found it intriguing that the minute I questioned her answer she had little faith in her answer.

I thought that I had learned to do this, but obviously I still need practice. During one math lesson, a student asked me why I only questioned wrong answers. I made a point to question all answers. If you don't, the minute you question them, they know their answer is wrong. It takes students a while to get used to this, but once they do I believe it helps strengthen their understanding if they can tell you how they reached the answer in math or why they think something is true. One critical thing I have learned is to question wrong answers as well as right answers.

Students Actually Learn if We Just Tell Them

Something I learned recently is that it is hard to change someone's thinking. We did a probe about an apple in the dark. Students were given a scenario about an apple being in a room with no light. Students first self-negotiated and chose one of four answers and why they believed that was the correct answer. One answer was that you would not see the apple regardless how long you are in the room. The second choice was you would see the red apple after your eyes adjusted. The third choice was you'd see the apple after your eyes adjusted, but not the color. Fourth choice was that you'd only see the shadow of the apple after your eyes adjusted. The last choice was you would see an outline of the apple after your eyes adjusted. When I walked around the room, I found it interesting that only one person had chosen the correct answer- you wouldn't see the red apple no matter how long you stay in the room. We had already had a lab on light and researched what the experts said. They could tell me that light was needed to see objects, yet they weren't connecting that learning to this probe. I was somewhat baffled, but knew it would turn out all right in the end. However, I did wonder how our debate would go if most people had a similar idea, and the idea was wrong. Would there be any debate at all? Would the one student with the correct idea state her opinion when it was the opposite of everyone else in the class? We moved right along and started sharing ideas. I have found that if you give students time to talk they will talk. I have never had a problem with students talking. Most students like to share their ideas.

Fifth Grade Students in Action

Here is a real example from a science debate in my fifth grade classroom. They had completed a lab to answer the question "How does the Respiratory System Work?" Each group had made a working model of the respiratory system and then written a claim supported by evidence. The class was now sharing claims and holding a debate. During this discussion, two groups had opposite ways to inflate the lungs. Also, no one seemed to know what the organ in our bodies the bottom balloon represented. Names have been changed. Please notice I said nothing throughout the entire discussion, which lasted for thirty minutes. Math was the only thing that stops the debate!

Emily- No one really knows for sure what this (bottom balloon) really is. I agree with Katie. It doesn't matter what this is or that is, pointing to parts on their model.

Kate- It's just a model. It's not like were looking in our body.

Brad- I disagree. We have something that helps our lungs, but they're saying the bottom balloon doesn't matter.

Chris- So are you saying it matters because it's part of how it works?

Brad- Yes.

Chris- I agree with that.

Kate- I think the bottom balloon does matter. But I think the actual bottle doesn't matter.

Faith- If it doesn't matter what the parts of our model are, how are we going to figure out how the lungs work?

Cole- If you think the bottle is ribs, they- the ribs and lungs- don't work together. The ribs just protect the lungs. Lungs- ribs- two separate things!

Chris- So are muscles and bones, but they work together?

Mike- Are you sure about that?

Kate- I think the bottom balloon matters but we don't know what it is! The bottle is just a bottle.

Brad- So you're saying we have a bottle in our body?

Kate- No, I'm just saying it doesn't matter what it is.

Glenda- Why not?

Emily- I agree with Kate.

Kate- It's just a bottle. Why does it have to represent something?

Knowing When to Stay Out of the Conversation

As you read above, I didn't have a part in their debate. This wasn't always the case, and it didn't start out easy. We as teachers want to be in control. It is after all our classroom. We are the teacher, and it is our job to teach our students, right? I have found that if we add our two cents into the debate then our students think what we say is true. That might prevent them from sharing what they are thinking, especially if it is different from what we stated.

It has taken me six years to feel comfortable letting students take the lead and debate without me. It's not that I never speak, but I have learned when it is appropriate and when it might hinder the conversation between students.

So when do you as the teacher jump into the debate? If so many students are talking at once, I will enter the conversation to remind students that only one may speak at a time. I had jumped in when I thought students needed some time to "chill out" and think for a minute. Sometimes our debates get pretty heated. When a student starts to get defensive, I jump in to remind them that we are disagreeing with an idea and not the person. I also might pose a question if I feel students are missing something valuable or if we have gotten off on a tangent.

I have also learned that some of the best debates can come from a tangent. It's hard to know when to bring them back to the main topic, but it's OK to let them share what they know. It's all a matter of the teacher's comfort level. After six years, I am comfortable with letting them veer off track a little. In my first few years, I would have jumped right in and brought them back to focus on the topic. I felt insecure or I was losing control of my class. There are still many times when I want to add a comment, but I just wait for a student to make that point. Usually if I wait long enough a student will say what I wanted to and I would much rather it come from a student.

HOW TO ADD WRITING TO SCIENCE CLASS

Pause and Reflect

This is a writing strategy I recently starting using. During our debate I have certain students who dominate the discussion, and I have others that feel they can't jump in and give their opinion. Or at times during the debate it was obvious that there are two or three main ideas about one concept. This is when I use what I call pause and reflect. It is just what it sounds like. Students pause from verbally giving their ideas and take time to reflect or self-negotiate. They retrieved their science journals and began to write. This was a great opportunity to let everyone have a voice. Sometimes I gave the class a question or topic to write about, like "What is the color of blood?" Other times I just asked them to reflect on what they heard that day. It is a timely tool to use if we are in the middle of a serious debate but need to stop due to time. Students read their reflection at the beginning of our next science class. Students used to grumble when I would ask them to stop and pause and reflect. But now I think more of the students like it, especially the timid ones who don't have a chance to jump in the conversation and add what they are thinking. As a teacher I like this strategy because it reinforces the writing aspect of science. It shows students that writing is a form of communicating our ideas. Some students can share their ideas easier on paper.

Reflections

At the end of a lab, I ask students to write a reflection of how their ideas changed over the course of the lab and what they learned. This is metacognition or thinking about your thinking. Students self-negotiate to think about how their thinking changed. Students think back about their ideas in the beginning, throughout, and now. This is why it is vital to have each student write their beginning ideas and to take time to pause and reflect throughout the unit. Students can go back and read what they were thinking. Metacognition is not an easy task and some kids struggle, but it is so essential to be able to put on paper what is going on in your head. I do not use this as a time for students to point out who was right and who was wrong. I stress that these reflections are to show our learning throughout the lab and unit.

Create a Page of Non-fiction Text

I use this occasionally at the end of a lab as a different way to assess if students understand the main points from the lab. It is a different way to have kids negotiate meaning. Earlier in the year we looked through non-fiction texts and made a list of all the different text features authors used. I connect that language skill to science writing. Students are asked to create one page of non-fiction text using text features we discussed. This text would show what they learned from the lab. Some of the students that were not excited about writing reflections, quickly started this task. Some students even made more than one page! When everyone is done, we have a gallery walk and read each other's pages. It is time for a negotiation. I have heard students say they thought that the information another student had in their page of text was wrong. After a gallery walk, it was noticed two students had the same fact, but the number of minutes it took sunlight to reach Earth was different. This started a debate in my room. These students went back to their source, and one realized she had written the wrong number. This was all from the students. They knew to go back to the source as I had taught them. This would not have been as powerful if I as the teacher had pointed out the wrong fact or simply written a comment in that student's journal. The fact that a student pointed out the difference and then the students went back to the resources to settle the conflicting data was exciting.

Not Just for Science

After using the SWH approach for six years, I find myself using bits and pieces in other subject areas. Even though this approach is called the Science Writing Heuristic, it can be used in all subject areas. I want my students to question ideas, think critically, share their opinions, make connections, and support their claims throughout the day, not just in science class. Therefore I use claims and evidences in reading. I have written claims on a quiz or worksheet and asked students to provide evidence to support it. Talking and debating isn't just saved for science class, but woven into the entire day. In reading, we have literature circles over the novels we read. Students can easily hold a thirty-minute discussion over two chapters. It goes beyond the typical summary type discussion. They use some of the same language they use in science. Phrases like these are common- I don't agree with that! Why do you think that? That's not what I think!

Set Expectations Early

When students are allowed to discuss, and in my classroom are highly encouraged to, it happens naturally. One reason this happens in my classroom is because from day one it is my expectation. Students know they will be expected to give their opinion in my classroom and give reasons or evidence for what is said. In my classroom, we don't post rules, but instead we have rights and responsibilities. It is a student right to voice their opinion and a responsibility to listen to others ideas. I set up my classroom to encourage discussion. Again, my desks are seldom in rows, and some-times desks are even pushed aside so the chairs can be arranged in a circle. This makes student-to-student debate easier. In fact, the students ask me if they can arrange them in a circle during debates. It is hard for students to interact when desks are in rows. Simple things like the way the desks are arranged in your classroom can encourage or hinder student debate.

SUMMARY

If I had to summarize this chapter in just one sentence it would be "get students talking and writing." I may have a noisy classroom, but there IS learning taking place. Don't be afraid to give up a little control. What a student learns doesn't have to come from the teacher. Students learn by doing. Students learn from listening to their peers. Students learn by reading from experts and realizing what they thought they knew was incorrect. Students learn from talking to other students, students learn from writing.

I tell my students I am not the "giver of knowledge". I provide opportunities for learning and my students love science! I didn't hear that ten years ago. Students want to be involved in their learning. Students want to be engaged in the unit. Students want to share their knowledge on a subject.

One student wrote in my scrapbook this year- Thank you for making science my favorite subject instead of my least favorite subject. This statement made an impact on me because this is the same for me. Thanks to the SWH approach, science has changed from my least favorite subject to teach to my favorite subject to teach.

Michelle Harris
Anita Elementary School
Anita, IA

MICHELLE GRIFFEN

3. SCIENCE AND LITERACY

Reading, Writing, Speaking, Listening, and Viewing through Science

I am in charge of the kindergarten through fourth grade scientists and computer users in my building. I have a computer lab with 26 iMacs, and I also team teach in ten kindergarten through fourth grade classes. All in all, I teach 20 tech sessions a week and 28 science sessions a week. Whew!

Previously I taught 4–8 tech, 5th grade, 4th grade and 1st grade. I had been teaching first grade for about six years using the science writing heuristic the last five of those years. I was so inspired by the power of using the SWH approach in my classroom I also decided to get a master's degree in science education. Combining my SWH approach knowledge with everything I was learning through my master's degree gave me motivation. I took that and asked the building principal if he would consider letting me teach science kindergarten through fourth grade. I got the science job and the added responsibility of teaching classes in the computer lab. This means I have spent a year running from room to room helping little scientists, writers, readers, thinkers, speakers, and listeners. Yes, we did ALL of those by using the SWH approach!

First of all, since this was my first time taking on five grade levels, I can tell you implementing the SWH approach as a "special" teacher compared to implementing it in my full time first grade classroom was a challenge. When I was full time in my own classroom, I had the luxury of melding science into reading, writing, and math the entire day if needed. Now, I was team teaching with ten other teachers who had their own plans for the rest of their day. Many times the writing, thinking and listening pieces of SWH approach spilled over into technology classes. It was a reasonable fit since we used our tech tools to help us communicate our science thoughts and ideas and each other.

Secondly, using the SWH approach required a lot of trial and error when I was in my own first grade classroom. Using SWH approach in ten different classrooms seemed like all trial and error at some points. I was fortunate to have patient and encouraging teachers with which to work. It is essential to understand using the SWH approach requires all your expertise as a teacher at your grade level. The beginning SWH approach teachers need to know that it is so powerful once you are able to implement it well. Starting to use the SWH approach is like being on a ship at sea. Following the text book series and doing the demonstrations and lab provided is like sailing near the coast in sight of the lighthouse. Beginning SWH approach teachers are sailing to the middle of the ocean during a storm with the only light to guide them coming from the intermittent lightning strikes.

*B. Hand and L. Norton-Meier, (eds.), Voices from the Classroom: Elementary Teachers'
Experience with Argument–Based Inquiry, 25–33.*

Sounds pretty scary, doesn't it? Remember, you never will go anywhere exciting if you stay within sight of the lighthouse. I bet sailors learned a lot about sailing on a vessel, when they actually went somewhere. Were they scared? Probably. Was it exciting at times? I'd sure hope so. They went and discovered some surprising places! The journey may be rough but the reward of teaching for learning using the SWH approach is so worth the risk of sailing into the middle of the ocean during a storm. Let me describe for you some of surprising places I've been this sailing the rough uncharted seas of SWH approach and literacy with my kindergarten through fourth grade shipmates.

THE AMBIGUOUS TRIANGLE: WRITING CLEAR QUESTIONS, CLAIMS, AND EVIDENCE

Even though I'd been using SWH approach for five years, it was not until using it across grade levels did I understand how literacy and science could not exist on their own. One highlight on my rough trip was sailing through the Ambiguous Triangle of Questions, Claims, and Evidence with second, third, and fourth grades. The Ambiguous Triangle is not a pleasant place to be if you are a scientist trying to communicate your ideas to other scientists.

For example, the learning target for second grade was "Magnets transfer energy." As a class we developed some testable questions and wrote some procedures to try to answer these questions. Each group was performing different tests on their magnets. When they finished, I asked them if they could write a claim. Here are some of our claims as written by the second grade:

Magnets will transfer through body parts sometimes. It sticks to your ear and it's like our earrings.

We tested everything seven times and it worked.

These claims are fine if you had been in the classroom and participated in the entire experience. I needed a captain to take charge of the vessel for a while and get us on a better course out of the triangle. As a class we shared claims, and I began asking questions.

"So, you tested everything seven times, and it worked? Hmm, let see it how it worked." I then took the stylus and wrote on the board and proclaimed joyfully, "It worked!" Then I walked over and hit the undo button and erased it and proclaimed with satisfaction, "Tah dah! It worked again! I bet you were right! EVERYTHING does work!"

Of course, this brought out protests such as, "No, we tested the magnets!"

"Well, you did not state you tested magnets, you stated you tested EVERY-THING!"

I demonstrated a couple more claims in the same fashion, then we were ready to discuss how to write a great claim anyone who is not in our science class can under-stand. I had told them the fourth graders had the same problems. The fourth graders decided:

– A good claim needs to mention the big idea.
– A good claim needs to be specific to the test.

Since I am teaching kindergarten through fourth grade, I decided I wanted to use the same language throughout. However, I did tell all the classes we might add or change our criteria list as needed and share it with everyone.

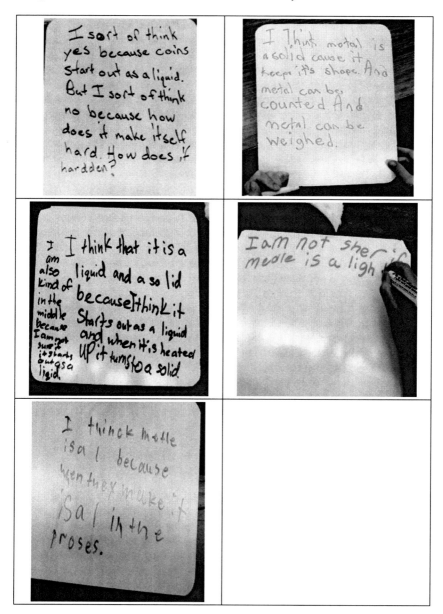

Figure 3-1. Students make initial claims on white boards.

The second grade class went through each scientist's claim and decided in groups if they were good claims based upon our criteria. When were then able to use the criteria to rewrite our claims and make them better. So, "Magnets will transfer through body parts sometimes. It sticks to your ear and it's like our earrings," was changed to "Small donut magnets will transfer energy through thin body parts, like our ear lobes." The students became more specific and precise in the wording of their claims.

I made the decision to critique all the questions, claims, and evidence with the entire class. I found the students learned more from the mistakes of each other and evaluating many questions, claims, and evidence gave everyone more practice than just working only on their groups' claims. Learning how to listen to and accept constructive criticism is just as important as learning how to evaluate and give constructive criticism. I also think making their drafts public made them realize how important social learning was to improving their product.

We were becoming better writers able to communicate our ideas using science. This year I found we sailed into the Ambiguous Triangle quite a bit the first half of the year. However, by using our criteria together as a class and in groups, the class was getting better and better at sailing around the Triangle with each science concept we tackled. I would often remind them of our first attempts at science writing, and they would all agree they were getting better. How powerful! The students were able to SEE and ASSESS their own ability to write clearly using authentic science work. They began to negotiate their learning privately and publicly.

One intense debate in third grade was centered on the question of whether or not metal was a liquid or a solid. They had previously been discussing the five states of matter (Bose-Einstein Condensate, solid, liquid, gas, and plasma) and their experiences with water as a solid, liquid, and gas when someone asked about metal. One of the strategies their teacher and I used was asking the students to make an initial claim and statement on their white boards (See Figure 3-1). The third grade teacher noticed how many third grade students wrote their claims clearly and in complete sentences. Did we tell them their claim had to be a complete sentence? No, they have begun writing clear and complete sentence automatically, even when they are writing for themselves. Wow!

THE CAPE OF CONTENTION: BECOMING GREAT LISTENERS, THINKERS, VIEWERS, AND SPEAKERS

I think one of the students' favorite places to sail is to the Cape of Contention. It is also the place where I feel my students have experienced the most learning. Every science concept is debated in the classroom using the students' questions claims and evidence, and expert knowledge. Sailing around the Cape of Contention required explicit sailing lessons. The lessons included how to listen to others, think about how their ideas compare, and then share their thoughts. They also learned how illustrating their ideas were helpful for their own and others' understanding. Again the students are continually negotiating publicly and privately throughout the lesson.

After seeing the initial claims, we begin by having students gather in the room with others who have the same claim as they do. Then the teacher and I stand back and let them debate their claims. As the students listen to others, they are free to change their minds and move to another group if they have been persuaded.

The students have been explicitly taught how to be a good listener, speaker, and thinker during our debates. At the beginning of the year, the same few students would debate, now our debates have started in small groups and overtaken the entire class as each group was using the illustrations on the interactive white board to make their case. Several times, this time included, the recess bell rang and they wanted to continue right on through recess. One student stopped me in the grocery store and he said, "That was a great argument we had today wasn't it?"

There have only been a couple occasions this year when the class has remained divided even after we have tested the concept and checked with the experts. This was an excellent time to learn about the nature of science. In our unit about landforms, they learned even scientists disagreed on the how some landforms came into being. Until new evidence is presented, disagreements may last for a long time.

Teaching how to participate in passionate science argument requires explicit teaching in every area of literacy. This year we focused on being a good thinker and listener. During one debate on the energy flow through the food web, the class was evenly divided in half, and each side was beginning to repeat their initial claims and reasons over and over again. The teacher and I stopped the class and had them write down the initial claim and reason of someone who disagreed with them. Then we asked them to think about what parts of the claim they agreed or disagreed with and why.

The process of writing their debates claim allowed many of the students to realise they were essentially stating the same thing only using different language. We discussed how good thinkers need to listen and consider ideas from another's point of view. Then they can make a decision or form an opinion about their claim. Just as the fourth graders agreed upon writing criteria for a good claim, the third graders were agreeing on the language they would use to express their ideas about energy flow in a food web.

Their teacher has explicitly taught paraphrasing authors and each other during reading time. During science time when these pre-taught skills would be needed he would remind them this was a time to use certain skills. Before we knew it, they began using these skills automatically just like they began using better writing skills automatically. Teaching literacy skills and providing relevant authentic experiences in which to use those skills allows students to experience learning beyond basic knowledge and recall. Science had become a meaningful endeavor to the students where they valued and wanted to improve their literacy skills. Science was answering the question many literacy teachers hear from their students, "Why do I have to learn this?"

After the class became deadlocked in their ideas about the food web, we checked with the experts by watching a video aimed at high school ecology students. I told them before watching the movie it was for high school students and once student said, "So that means we won't understand anything." I said, "We'll see." I watched as students' faces brightened up and they started raising their hands in the air to state, "We know that! And that! And that!" They were very proud of themselves. I said, "See, you understand that video. Why do you think it was easy to understand?" "Well, we talked and talked and talked about the food chain and food web every day."

I reminded them they also wrote about the concepts in the movie, learned about the Latin parts of words such as –vore, omni-, cani- etc., "And we had good arguments didn't we?" They are proud of their debating ability!

What their teacher and I did not do was teach vocabulary. The students *did not* do vocabulary worksheets or memorize vocabulary words. However, by listening to our students and reading their writing, you would never know it. By engaging in authentic science activities, they used these words over and over to communicate with each other. We would introduce the words as needed when they came up in their conversations. For example, in first grade they had just learned what matter was by watching a video. The video also mentioned mass and volume. Two concepts the third graders initially struggled with in the beginning.

BATTEN DOWN THE HATCHES: WRITING AND DRAWING TO
RECORD DATA AND FOLLOW PROCEDURES

Sometimes sailors just plain forget to batten down the hatches. It is the little things sailors must remember to do correctly in order to weather storms or sail smoothly along. I found students needed help understanding the importance of data collection and following procedures.

The first graders were comparing masses and volumes of cotton balls and cubes using balances. Which side of the balance had more volume? Which side of the balance had more mass? These two questions we discussed over and over and over. When I felt they were pretty comfortable with the terms, they were told to find any two items in the class they thought had different masses. They put both items on the balance and recorded their data. They then had to make a claim about the items mass and volume and share it with the group. This activity was a good time for the first graders to practice listening to each other to decide whether they thought the claim being made was correct or not. If the claim was in the debate, we asked to see their data. "Uh-oh, you forgot to draw you scale or write down a math problem using greater than and less than?"

This was the first time first graders, even the most reluctant writers, realized their science writing was very, very important. I very nicely explained, "We don't have time to retest your objects today. So, we won't be able to evaluate your claim. I'm sorry; I hope you remember to write down your data next time." Their ship was docked in the harbor. RATS! It only took a couple of times of not being able to share their evidence because they lacked data before many first graders began writing the word DATA on their data page and made sure they were recording their data.

A lot of writing in first grade is accomplished as a class. They did an experiment where they mixed a solid and a liquid. We wrote the procedure together for the first experiment. This gave them another opportunity to use vocabulary such as solid, liquid, and volume. They also learned how to measure volume-using milliliters. Unfortunately, some students ran their ship into the rocks. Instead of using the procedure we had written, they were doing the experiment willy-nilly. Many solids and liquids were declared contaminated and dumped down the sink.

They had a similar experience when it came to comparing their repeat of the solid/ liquid experiment when they forgot to write the date on each data page. First graders do have some difficulty using their notebooks and often they get pages out of order. When they had to write about their experiment, some could not remember which test was first. These experiences of not writing important information down and also, not following the procedure we developed, really helped the first graders to realize the important role writing, reading, and thinking plays in science.

Writing became relevant in the science classroom The first graders were realizing why writing was so important and not just something they HAD to do because they teacher asked them too. Making learning relevant and authentic to students had reached even the most reluctant students.

GOOD SAILORS CHECK THE WEATHER: USING WRITING TO READ
AND SPEAKING, VIEWING AND LISTENING TO LEARN

Just as a good captain would check on the weather ahead, I began the weather unit by asking the kindergartners to help me list all the weather words in which they were familiar. Each section came up with about thirty words. This did give me some idea of their prior knowledge, one section began talking about how they had a relative in Arizona, and they had different winter weather than in Iowa. Good information to know.

I then took these words and paired each one with a picture. We then used these words in our weather journal. The picture paired with the word made if very easy for students to find the word they wanted to use in their journal. They even began drawing pictures to go with other words we added on the chalkboard as we learned about them. They realized the words and pictures were linked. They even began finding some of their weather words in other books and worksheets. Some students were acquiring some weather words as part of their sight word list.

Each science day we would write the date on the top of the page. It was a momentous occasion when they began to realize the date or name of the month was in other locations around the room too! Then, guess what? They also had weather words on their calendar too! They were very excited when recognizing and valuing print for the first time.

Because I teach two sections of kindergarten, my second time through a lesson seemed to go smoother, because I was more prepared for students' ideas and misconceptions. Therefore, the second group had more time to write. At the end of the unit, I tested both sections on how well they could read their weather words. The groups that did more writing were able to read 12 percent more weather words. This is a powerful lesson for me. Next year I need to have students write more.

As with the older students, I did not spend any time drilling vocabulary words. Every science class for weeks we went outside and checked the "precipitation, visibility, clouds-stratus, cirrus, and cumulus, wind direction and force, sunshine, and temperature..." I'd have little kindergarten scientists asking over and over again at recess to check the temperature etc. One recess was spent debating over clouds. "I think it looks like stratus clouds." "No, they are cumulus, see the tops." "But over there it looks like cirrus." This went on for a while and then they asked me to settle the argument. I told them they I agreed with all of them and they were silent for a bit. Then I began asking each one why they thought they labeled the clouds the way they did. After the first two explained another said, "Oh, so we can have sometimes different lots of clouds!"

This year I learned kindergarteners had some interesting ideas as to the origin of precipitation. Exactly two, TWO, kindergartners said precipitation came from clouds. The rest suggested God, Jesus, Mother Nature, and the sky. How surprising! For the first time, I believe the kindergartners were interested in what the other students had to say. After one suggestion, the rest looked very thoughtful and contemplative. This question was definitely causing them to think and take a risk by sharing their answers. I think they were more surprised when I told them I was not giving the answer, and they would have to ask someone else.

We then talked about whom we could ask. Most said they would ask their parents. I asked them if they thought their parents would know. Silence and thoughtful looks followed. I asked them if they thought the preschoolers would know. Would babies know? Of course not! Many suggested asking their teacher. I asked them what they would do if no one knew. No one knew. Hmm! What do you think a scientist would do?

They responded, "A scientist would just go outside and look..."

"Yeah!"

Then I said, "Could we go look now?"

"Yeah!"

"Wait, is there any precipitation outside now?"

"No! Now what?"

"We have to wait for some rain or something."

"Is rain the only kind of precipitation?"

"What do you think he means when he said it is only rain now."

This brought on a lot of conversation.

Even though science arguments were more difficult for me in kindergarten, I'm slowing sailing that boat out of the storm. I need to hone my questioning skills and remember to have them share their ideas with a partner or their table groups. I do hope our conversation about the origin of precipitation made them think about checking their ideas with science experts I also hope they realize they can think and figure things out too!

PREPARING FOR THE NEXT TRIP

It was a rough trip this year, but I did enjoy it. I am already looking forward to next year. I learned this year the students learned so much from using their vocabulary words in their writing, listening, and speaking, I plan on doing all the physical science first. So much of physical science is interwoven into the other sciences. Students constantly need to consider physical properties of matter when they are running tests. Do all our variables have the same mass and volumes? Is the water in this test all the same temperature? What properties can we ignore? Does it matter if one can is metal and the other can is plastic? Using the vocabulary of learned through physics over and over continually will be valuable.

Another teacher and I are working on concept maps around the big idea of how literate students listen. We want to teach how great listeners focus, think and respond when hearing directions, persuasive arguments, information, or entertainment. All these can be used during science. Since I am in all rooms and she works with Kindergarten through second grade, we thought visual reminders for us and the students will help us remember to teach these important skills.

Our science classes began to become much more powerful when the students knew what they were to focus on and think about while someone was talking. Previously, I spent time on what good listening looked like from the perspective on the speaker. I never, not once, help children realize what good listeners thought about while they were listening. I never told them how to decide the speaker's purpose. Sure, we practiced identifying facts and opinions, but what would students do when you are not sure the speaker's information is valid? I never taught them to evaluate the speaker's credentials. For some kids, this might come naturally, but for many kid's it is not. One debate about the adaptations of a certain fish was at a standstill when someone in the group said, "Let's ask Hailey about that fish. That was the fish she studied in the computer lab." He realized they had an expert in their room. She even printed the information out about the fish. The group was able to evaluate each other's knowledge, and they realized they needed to find an expert. This class had realized the value of working together and sharing knowledge. Their class became their own personal learning network.

The beauty of sailing the SWH ship is not only the times where encounter smooth waters, but also the times where the sailing is rough or when we run the ship ashore. Those are the times the students get to practice and improve on their literacy skills. If we want them to be literate in reading, writing, listening, thinking, and speaking, we need to give them plenty of authentic challenges where they can use these skills. Worksheets and made-up scenarios, all of which I have tried at one time or another, do not present opportunities for literacy. The SWH approach does. They get to practice these skills, such as using vocabulary words and doing something they care about because SWH approach is student centered. They can evaluate their own growth from unit to unit. As they become better with each challenge, they value their literacy skills even more.

The SWH approach made my students better in all facets of literacy. Reading is the part of literacy teachers teach well, however, it is one part. My students not only became better readers, but also improved their listening skills, thinking skills, viewing, and speaking skills. A student needs ALL of these pieces to become a literate student. The SWH approach ensures students will be using and practicing all these pieces at a *higher order thinking* during each science class to keep the ship afloat.

Do not be afraid to sail off into the great big ocean. There might be rough seas, but what an adventure! Remember, one day our students will go sailing their own ship. What kind of sailor will they be if we never took them out beyond the reach of the lighthouse?

Michelle Griffen
Riverside Community School District
Carson, Iowa, USA

AMY HIGGINBOTHAM AND CHRISTINE SUTHERLAND

4. WRITING FOR A REASON

A Primary Purpose to Write

SWH is like dessert! We like to have it with every meal, crave it with every subject. It is what we look forward to. Unlike dessert, SWH is beneficial throughout the day. We consume large amounts and gain nothing but knowledge and experience. It is not an extra that you do not need and must prepare in addition to the main dish. It is teaching for understanding and learning with a purpose.

WHEN DO WE WORK ON SCIENCE

In a typical classroom, science is 20–30 minutes long during a routine time of the day. With the SWH approach, evidence of science is happening all day long. Science time used to be the first thing cut with the increasing demands placed on teachers to teach reading and math.

Although we have a designated time for the SWH approach, it tends to creep into just about every other part of the day. Science negotiations are not intended for a particular time in the day but occur as a result of what is noticed as we listen to student conversations. These discussions are crucial to enable students to feel like *scientists* in our classrooms. When learning time is as student-centered as possible, the students are most successful. Discussions are most effective when occurring naturally throughout the course of the day. Negotiations require tolerance and energy as students at this young age are highly active and have a range of attention spans and learning styles. Ideas are often noted in some form for further discussion during SWH time. We look forward to SWH because throughout the day we find ideas in our reading, writing and discussion that we add to our concept map or list of questions. Students often choose to write about science topics because science writing is purposeful writing based on real experiences, learning and thinking. We draw, label and write with a purpose; Writing in science emerges naturally.

TOUR OF THE SWH PRIMARY CLASSROOM

You will most likely see something different in each of our classrooms, even though our goals are the same. Some days we are working in laboratories, artist's studios, stages, publishing companies, construction sites, weather stations, day spas, or what-ever is necessary to the students and their learning. Science and the SWH approach are in everything we do. SWH can be seen through evidence of a big idea, concept maps,

B. Hand and L. Norton-Meier, (eds.), Voices from the Classroom: Elementary Teachers' Experience with Argument–Based Inquiry, 35–47.

questions that have been recorded, non-fiction texts, resources on specific topics, and hands-on materials that support investigations. A visitor to the classroom can immediately identify the learning goal.

Our classrooms are not places where you can find lesson plan books that have been filled out weeks in advance. The children and their ideas determine daily what will happen next. In place of page numbers and worksheets are sticky notes and references to resources that are needed to research and investigate. The voices of children are even recorded in lesson plans. Questions, questions, questions, are the key to the SWH approach. By carefully listening to questions, we are able to record what it is we need to study and then the fun begins.

In many ways, the concept map has become our lesson plan, posted for students to use as both a reference for writing and a map of opportunities for us to learn and explore (See Figure 4-1). The plan for learning is no longer in the teacher's hands but is a work in progress on the wall. Concept maps are clearly posted and placed in an area in which they can be referred to during large group discussions. Concept maps may include but are not limited to pictures, words, and ideas that link together. Everything that is on the concept map is student generated. All words are recorded as evidence of what kids are thinking, even if everyone does not agree. It is, in fact, disagreements that lead to further questions. The concept map brings the group together to review the big idea and share their thinking. The big idea is clearly posted and referred to no matter which direction the learners go or what discoveries are made along the way. The big idea begins as the center of the concept map and students are pre-assessed on questions related to the big idea. The discoveries, even though they may be individual, will in some way be represented through the big idea on the concept map.

During our study of weather, students begin to share weather types. The teacher records the weather types on the concept map. Much to her surprise, earthquake is

Figure 4-1. Students use the concept map to find words that describe a toy they are writing about.

accepted as a weather type, and she records it on the map next to rain, wind, snow, sun and cloudy. When a student suggests rainbow as a type of weather, several hands go up, and negotiations begin as to where rainbow belongs on the concept map. Are rainbows sun, rain or both? Unlike the word earthquake, which is written with no argument, rainbow must be put temporarily above rain and sun to reflect the claims being made by students. One student claims, "A rainbow is a reflection of the sun. Put it with sunny." The teacher notes the word reflection, so we can revisit this term another time. Another child claims it must go with rain because it comes after it rains. Finally, a third student asks, "Isn't a rainbow sun and rain mixed together?" The teacher begins to think of questions and investigations that will help the class negotiate learning about rain and sun. This discussion leads naturally to a list of questions about weather. A list of questions guides the instruction. Questions about rainbows are added to the list. The teacher reviews what is added to the map and shares her question about earthquakes. "Is earthquake a type of weather?" Many students say yes, some say no and a few do not respond. The teacher records her question on the list and shares her thoughts; "What is weather?" Students respond with weather words from the map. No one says earthquake. The teacher asks, "How are snow and rain the same?" "Where do we see the sun and the clouds, let's think about this."? These questions need to be answered through investigations. We invite experts to share what they know about weather (and earthquakes); we have discussions, read books, watch videos, set up experiments and record data to help us construct knowledge about weather. The transition from presenting information in ways we believe are effective to asking questions to find out how students are thinking is challenging. It can be a struggle to leave understanding where it is on the map instead of sharing knowledge. There is a fine line between giving students the information and creating wonder through questioning and investigation opportunities for students to negotiate their own understanding.

CONCEPT MAPS HELP STUDENTS WRITE

Next to the concept map is a place to list questions that come up from discussions and review using the concept map. All questions are recorded to validate individual thinking. These questions play a key part in the setup of hands-on materials and non-fiction text needed to encourage, inspire and support learning on a variety of levels. Students record their ideas, observations and findings in journals, student-made books, or on plain white paper. This written material is used to share their ideas with others so that they may enjoy or learn.

Non-fiction books related to the big idea are placed in an area separate from the classroom library and are used frequently by both the teacher and students (See Figure 4-2). These books are models for students to learn to write like real scientists and find answers to their questions. Teachers also use the non-fiction texts to read-aloud and to model their thinking during reading. When reading to learn about the big idea, text features are often critical to the learning and can provide ample opportunities for direct instruction. Students use the text features both as a reader and a writer. An example of this is the discovery that the table of contents means students do not have to read an entire book to answer one question.

Figure 4-2. These students are reading to learn and recording important vocabulary relating to outer space. The student goal is to work together to write a book titled: The ABC's of outer space.

Centers are student-centered with an outcome that is determined by the students rather than the teacher. ***Centers*** are not pre-determined but evolve out of questions and learning that occurs as the units unfold. For example, a rock-sorting center was created using egg cartons and rocks students brought in along with several from other faculty members. Books created by the class during a senses study become a popular center. Following our study of properties of objects students repeat tests with magnets and objects that sink or float.

TAKE A LOOK AT HOW THIS ALL BEGAN

When speaking on how we began it is important to reflect on where we are. SWH is not a strategy that we use only at a specific time or ideas from a book that we incorporate occasionally. It is a way of thinking and learning that has allowed us to continue to learn and grow so that students may learn and grow. In all that we do professionally and personally as learners we are affected by the SWH approach.

Our training began as a week long opportunity to negotiate meaning of the approach through hands-on investigations as if we were students learning new science concepts. We were asked to think about thinking. Rather than being told how to use the SWH approach we were expected to investigate, make claims and ask questions. As we begin each year we reflect on building our own understanding and use that experience to ease students into a new way of thinking. We remember the impact of asking questions, especially asking "why". We begin the school year intending to teach students to read and write and to try to integrate science. We end the year having explored science concepts we never dreamed we would have in kindergarten. Through the integration of science and writing we learn that students can write like real scientists. Along the way, we cannot wait to talk to our peers about the ideas and thinking going on in our classroom.

We spend time collaborating, planning big ideas and making cross-curricular connections and then the school year begins. We want to get started right away, but there is so much to do the first few weeks of school with new kindergartners. The year begins with brand new school supplies and procedures, to teach and learn. These supplies and procedures become the materials for our first ideas, questions, tests, observations, claims, evidence and reflections. Many ideas help students build under-standing of our first big idea: objects can be described by their properties. We use our school supplies and classroom environment as tools for investigation. We begin to create a community of learners making instant applications to improve our class-room learning environment. We sort materials and find places in the room to store them. We investigate several different types of crayons and discover similarities and differences, not only in color but also size and performance. This investigation requires paper, which leads to investigations on different types of paper. A system for organizing paper by size and color is established. Decisions are made on which type of paper is best for crayons, markers and paint. Throughout the year, students reference our investigations as they make decisions about completing assignments with crayons or markers. It is decided that two sided projects are best suited for crayons because markers show through the paper. The student's choices are based on their own thinking rather than looking to the teacher to set rules and expectations. We have found that students are more organized and efficient when they are making their own decisions based on questions, claims and evidence.

Along the way, we make several changes (formerly called mistakes). Changes are made throughout the year based on student experiences with supplies. The need to test markers and crayons before adding them to student crayon boxes leads students to try them out. In the past, this would have been approached as a mistake made by students. Now it is looked at as an investigation resulting in a change in how our classroom is set up. The question is posted, "How can we test markers and crayons without making a mess?" Students can be seen testing markers before taking them to a project. Both paper and a dry erase board are now located near these items for that specific purpose. Kids are just waiting to test all those new supplies, now we can harness that curiosity and guide them to use what they have learned from these investigations. Beginning the year with an inquiry approach to supplies and procedures has created a climate where students are in charge of their learning. They do not wait for instruction to come from the teacher. They test ideas and ask questions.

WHAT KIDS CAN DO!

We have learned to ask questions that lead to higher level thinking and then ask more questions. We notice that by asking questions, our students ask additional questions.

Our lesson plans for the next day depend on the thinking that occurs today. We listen to the conversations of children. Each child believes their thinking is important to what will happen in the classroom. Much of our planning for the next lesson develops within classroom discussions. Minimal planning time is spent without student input.

All students are encouraged to contribute, and their comments are valued. Students with stronger knowledge are given higher level questions; for example, a stronger reader is encouraged to explain his thinking and how he found his idea by reading information from a chart in the room. Less accomplished students are often supported with practices such as, whispering to someone next to you, repeating and rephrasing ideas, and additional opportunities to think aloud. Repetition and different modalities provide the scaffolding students need. Students can participate in science writing in a variety of ways. In kindergarten interactive writing supports the science thinking of students that may struggle with writing on their own.

Many students respond to music as a means to express themselves and to help them remember. Using science understandings to create new song lyrics for familiar songs often gives students an exciting purpose to participate in writing. An example of this begins with a verse created to reflect our discoveries about wind:

Here comes the wind, here comes the wind, and I say it is blowing.

Wind, wind, wind, it is air moving.

The result of the investigation of rainbows became:

Here comes the rain, here comes the sun, and I say it is a rainbow.

Rain and sun make a rainbow!

Listening to students sing the lyrics throughout the day and try to create new verses on their own helps with the planning for future reflections on weather. Kids know what they want to learn and how they learn best.

WRITING FOR A PURPOSE

One of our greatest struggles as primary teachers is to get young children to take risks and write to the best of their ability. This is beginning to change, as we gain experience with SWH. We approach writing and science in the same way. We give students the opportunity to write, share their writing and receive feedback, which can be powerful to the young writers.

One way of providing a purposeful writing opportunity is by having the students share a writing project with others. For the weather unit, students create a weather diorama with their families. When they bring it to school, they are asked to share it with another student/class. During this sharing time, they ask for other ways the weather might affect us. As students return to the class with their dioramas, they report any new information, and we note it on our concept map. Before sending the dioramas home, students design a certificate for each diorama to recognize the specific understanding this project brings to our class. An award is created for two sunny weather dioramas showing us how temperature affects the activities we do outside and how we dress. Another student commends the students' use of animals to show how weather also affects animals. The purpose emerges because of the interest and appreciation of the students' work and the desire to acknowledge this effort before letting the dioramas go home. As a result, students reflect on what they learn about weather and make an extra effort to write neatly because the format of the writing is a special certificate.

During our unit on the five senses, students design a brochure for our Feel Good Spa (See Figure 4-3). The brochure is designed to record findings we investigate using each of our five senses. Students invite a faculty member to our spa and use the brochure to share what they are learning. Students ask questions to find out how others use their five senses to enjoy the world.

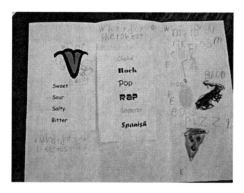

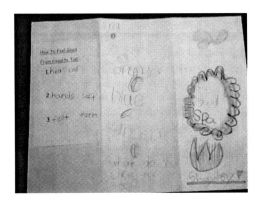

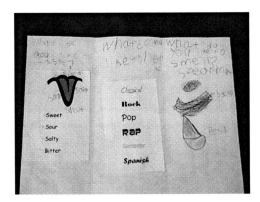

Figure 4-3. Student brochures for the five senses study.
The classroom became a feel good spa.

It is important to be flexible with content but true to inquiry. Kids have ideas about what they want to learn. With guidance, they create questions, investigations and negotiations that help them build understanding that is meaningful and useful.

Staying true to inquiry allows student knowledge to build. When students get what they need to know when they need to know it, they transfer the knowledge and gain more understanding. Evidence of this is shown in a classroom activity, with the intent of just planting seeds to see what happens (See Figure 4-4). The investigation evolves into making claims about what will grow. We use resources to figure out what type of seeds they are and what a marigold and zinnia will look like. This requires a leaf comparison and several discussions about student experiences with plants and gardening. Having our Mother's Day plants die would have been a problem in the past. SWH turns situations like this into investigations with deeper understanding.

About halfway through the school year we notice the most amazing thing happening in our classrooms. Our students are writing, writing, writing (See Figure 4-5). They walk into the room in the morning asking, "Can I make a book?" On the way to school students make plans to co-author a book with a friend and have topics and word banks that they have prepared at home. We have trouble finding enough time in each day to share the books they have written. This is a result of SWH and the thinking involved in our learning experiences. Children are not coming to school to be fed knowledge. They walk in the door with the natural imagination and curiosity of a child, and they use leadership and collaboration skills to effectively communicate their ideas.

Today's math practice is an example of how the SWH approach impacts other areas of the curriculum. We provide direct instruction on computation with a focus on subtraction. The students are instructed to notice and use key vocabulary related to subtraction, and they have opportunities to practice using manipulatives and math worksheets. In preparation for conferences, we ask students to create their

Figure 4-4. A student writes directions for planting a seed successfully on the back of a seed packet.

Figure 4-5. This student writes with a clear purpose to inform his readers.
He uses specific vocabulary, detailed illustrations and labels.

own subtraction stories and record the equations. In previous lessons, we had only practiced subtraction numbers up to ten. When given the open-ended task to create their own stories students subtract double-digit numbers and explain their thinking. Students are observed writing number stories in the book making center and use books from the math tub to get ideas such as using rhyming words. ***Students of varying abilities are setting goals for themselves that reach far above what the kindergarten curriculum provides.*** When students participate in the reading center, it is not simply because it is their day to attend. Students are reading with a vision for the writing they are going to do.

WRITING AND THE YOUNG CHILD

We are not planning writing projects anymore. Students develop the need to write. Students work in smaller groups with a variety of books they think may have the answer to a specific question. As a group, they look through the books and sticky note pages they believe have information that will be helpful to the large group.

The teacher provides support mainly through listening, questioning and at times by providing direct instruction on reading strategies or text features. Next, students record their findings from the text. The purpose for this writing is to bring information to the group. As students use books, they read, reread, ask questions and write using a published text as a model. The students have a specific audience in mind when writing. Students will read their own writing and know that their peers will read their writing as well. Students want to choose information that supports their thinking and will perhaps change the thinking of others. This is powerful writing even though students are not producing the words all by themselves.

The SWH approach makes a difference in the way we conference with students about how they write. The conferences are more productive because students are used to being asked about their thinking. Selecting text to support student writing is done after conferencing with kids about their ideas. In conferencing with a child struggling to explain her idea the teacher says, "I will order books about rockets for Ben, what type of books would help you with your writing?" The student replies, "I really want to make people think when they read my book." The teacher continues, "Well what type of books make us think?" The student replies, "We have read some riddle books that made me think!" With more questioning and conversation, the student is excited to begin writing a riddle book about food (See Figure 4-6). Kids want to add what they have learned about science concepts to their writing. Authentic discussions about fiction vs. nonfiction text emerge during our conference. We find students making claims about their writing and supporting their claims with evidence to help their audience believe their ideas or enjoy the book.

Figure 4-6. The student used a prior experience as a reader to write
a riddle book about food.

When asked to draw a picture of a plant that we planted for Mother's Day, students add details to their drawing and begin writing descriptively without being prompted (See Figure 4-7). As Mother's Day approaches, our study of what type of container would be best for our plants becomes more urgent. Some of the plants are not doing so well. The teacher tells the students that she thinks the plants are not getting enough water because the egg cartons being used are made of cardboard. Before the class gets busy transplanting the plants into plastic cups the teacher asks, "What do you think?" The class erupts in conversation. Some think the egg cartons are too small, some say they did not water them enough, some say they did not get enough sun, and they need to put them outside. The students try different containers and as scientists, record their findings. A plain sheet of paper allows students to write about what is happening in a way that makes sense to them. Prior knowledge is activated when the discovery is made that the seeds have been planted in containers made of different materials (glass, plastic, porcelain, tin, and cardboard). Students record observations of plant growth. They use prior knowledge of properties of objects to make claims about the size and the material each container is made of. This approach truly gives students opportunities to construct their own knowledge!

Figure 4-7. Students used plant journals to record observations of seeds planted in the classroom. These journals were used to design a packet of seeds with instructions for growth on the back.

Within our weather unit, we use SKYPE as a tool to communicate from classroom to classroom within our building. Students share information they discover regarding temperature and how it affects students at recess. This is a highly motivating experience which allows students to make connections by understanding the significance of communicating with others. After sharing information on SKYPE, conversation continues at lunch and recess. This experience also leads to discussion and reflection between colleagues on which direction to go with further lessons. Curricular connections are made when we have the opportunity to SKYPE with a relative in Spain. She shares the temperature in a far away location and how that affects her and the environment. We are making maps of our classroom in Social Studies. Students are eager to get their hands on a world map to find the location of a far away country. From this experience, students bring maps from home that show where extended family members live. Several students write letters asking about weather in far away places.

SUMMARY AND FUTURE CHALLENGES

Teaching from an inquiry stance is ongoing, and we have to be open to accepting new ideas and challenges along the way. One of the challenges we face is being prepared for the diverse needs of the group. Making text available at the level our students are reading takes creativity and resourcefulness. It is amazing how motivating nonfiction text is when available at just the right time.

Collaboration with peers is challenging at times. Communication used to be a sharing of ideas or duplicating lessons from teacher to teacher. We are beginning to discover the power of students from one class collaborating with students from another class with the support of the teachers. One example of this is using SKYPE from one classroom to the other. Communication between classrooms is an eye opener as we recognize possibilities we now have when students are building their own knowledge. Talking with colleagues about conversations taking place in our classrooms and questions our students ask is more effective than sharing lesson plans.

It is easy to say students have misconceptions or misunderstandings. Sticking with this approach enables us to see that these are understandings and knowledge students have built based on their experiences and negotiations. As educators, it is our responsibility to find out how students have come to their understandings or knowledge and help them to acquire a deeper understanding. Changing their thinking with negotiations that are meaningful and building on their prior knowledge is our goal. Our biggest challenge is to continually be open to changing our own thinking right along with the students, and our previous experiences with the SWH approach assure us that we are up for the challenge!

Amy Higginbotham and Christine Sutherland
Lewis Central Community Schools
Council Bluffs, Iowa, USA

KIM WISE

5. LENS OF LEARNING IN THE SWH

It was messy. I knew from my previous visits, it had been noisy too. Words were written everywhere in different colors. Some words with bullets, some in bold print and some words so squished in they barely fit. Many things were crossed out. A few sections or words were circled. Posters layered on top of other posters. It was messy. I knew it had been noisy. To me it was a picture of excitement and of learning. (See Figure 5-1)

This teacher valued the voice of her students. The posters recorded the process of their learning. What did they think they knew? What questions did they have? What were they finding out from their investigations? How was their learning changing? Did some things now not make sense? Do they now have more examples? More questions? Student learning was visible to all as one looked around the walls of the classroom.

Images like the one described above are the reason I love my job. I get to witness learning in action—both from the perspective of the teacher and those of the students. It is never the same and it is never boring. The Science Writing Heuristic (SWH) approach has allowed teachers to rekindle their passion for teaching and therefore infused classrooms with the love of learning.

I am a science consultant for an area education agency in Southwest Iowa. As part of that job, I provide professional development to teachers around the SWH approach. I have been learning about the approach since 2002 and that learning will never cease. I'll never know enough. There will always be more questions that need to be answered. Those are two, of many reasons, that when I engage teachers around this approach, it never looks the same from semester to semester and certainly from year to year. What we knew when we first began implementing looks different than what we do today and I'm sure it will look different five years from now. Because of this constant deepening of understanding, my role is often that of a coach. How can we teachers move closer to that expanding definition of the SWH?

In my capacity as a professional developer, I work with many different groups of teachers. Some groups are small and are engaged in a book study of *Questions, Claims, and Evidence*. These groups meet monthly to reflect on a reading from the book and discuss their implementation efforts. Many groups are a part of a building or district professional development. Others are participants in research projects that have on-going training during the summer and weekends. Whatever the group, my role is to help them gain and strengthen an understanding of the approach through modeling, observations, feedback and consultations. Besides on-site training, I support teachers through phone calls, e-mails, and other electronic means such as Skype.

B. Hand and L. Norton-Meier, (eds.), Voices from the Classroom: Elementary Teachers' Experience with Argument–Based Inquiry, 49–59.

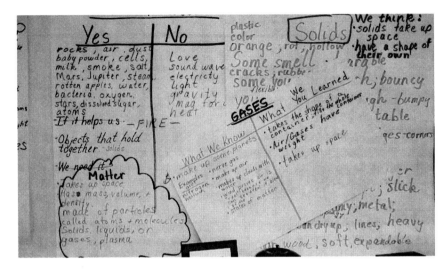

Figure 5-1. Evidence of learning in an SWH classroom.

Because the SWH is such a HUGE shift in a teacher's view of teaching and learning, support has to be on-going and frequent. The time and effort are immense, but the student success is so worth it!

When I'm supporting teachers I try to keep the same mindset that they use in the classroom: What do they know? What do they struggle with? How can I provide opportunities for them to gain the understanding they need to implement at an even higher level? This is my view of *assessment*. It isn't a grade. It isn't a judgment. It's data. It is a way for me to think about their progress and learning. It is a way for me to coach them to think about their progress and learning. Then, together, we can determine what can be done to help them, so the kids become more successful.

CONCEPTUAL UNDERSTANDING AND BIG IDEAS

When I speak to teachers or visit their classrooms, I'm looking and listening for many things to give me an idea of how they are doing with the SWH. One of the advantages of this approach is that teachers are never asked to change their curriculum. Whatever the district was using before implementation for standards and benchmarks can be used with this approach. As teachers learn more about inquiry and what it means to learn, I often receive a request to help them make their curriculum more conceptual. For example, simple machines or rockets are common units of instruction in intermediate elementary classrooms. Simple machines and rockets are only "vehicles" to help students understand the concept of force and motion. So my job is to help teachers see the difference between topics and concepts. Simple machines and rockets are topics. Force and motion is a concept. Now they can dig deeper into their concept. What about force and motion should EVERY student understand? As a result of these negotiations, teachers are often left with fewer concepts to address in a typical school year, which is more manageable than an entire textbook full of ideas!

Once teachers are aware of what they should be teaching during their school year, big ideas can be crafted. A big idea is a statement that reflects a standard and benchmark, uses kid-friendly language, and provides a focus for instruction. Big ideas normally have a single definition, but multiple pathways to that definition exist.

Everything that happens during a unit comes back to the big idea. Students should be able to answer the question—*how did today help me better understand the big idea?* It is essential to using this approach. Examples of big ideas include:
– Living things grow and change.
– Materials from the earth have special qualities that make them useful in different ways.
– Our senses help us understand the world.

Because of the importance of the big idea in focusing the teaching and learning, we ask teachers to post them in the classroom. (See Figure 5-2)

The posted big idea is something I can look for in a classroom. This helps start a conversation with a teacher (and if it is NOT there, that is something to talk about too!). I like to talk to a teacher about how the big idea was created. Is it based on a standard and benchmark? What does she know about the big idea? That's a big question for teachers. Most have not examined their own understanding of the big idea. This is scary at first, especially for elementary teachers. Many feel that they have to be the masters of many subjects, not just science. Due to this lack of confidence, science often takes lower priority in the classroom than literacy and math. SWH teachers see the power of the science big idea providing the home for the application of both literacy and math skills.

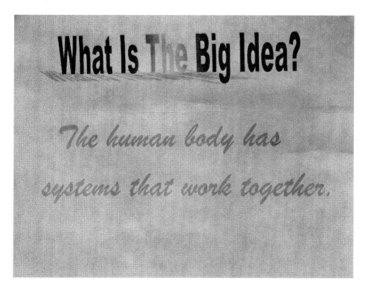

Figure 5-2. The big idea is posted in the classroom.

EXAMINING OUR OWN UNDERSTANDING

As teachers attend our professional development, we ask them to create a concept map showing their understanding of the big idea (See Figure 5-3). Reluctance would be an understatement! Some feel they don't know anything about the concept while some just refuse to consider this step might be purposeful for student learning. These comments are data to me. This illustrates to me their confidence in not only the content but the process. Teachers that implement this approach begin to feel more comfortable in how their own personal knowledge of the concept is still growing. They know that learning is so valued in an SWH classroom that their own questions will only strengthen the instruction. This works if the teacher is not afraid to say they don't know. By setting ourselves up in the classroom as the "holder of all correct knowledge" kids want to play the "guess what's in the head of the teacher" game. Trying to please the teacher by giving them back what they want to hear isn't learning– it is regurgitation.

The teacher concept map helps SWH teachers anticipate where kids might "enter" the concept. I hear that high implementing teacher's concept map creates a road map with all the various routes students might pursue to reach he big idea. The target never moves. The big idea doesn't change, but the journey each class or even individual learner takes might be slightly different. Teachers that embrace the SWH approach to learning are comfortable knowing their lesson plans might change day to day, and it may be impossible to plan weeks at a time. That's OK, because they know learning at a deeper level is happening for their kids and the teacher concept map supports that claim.

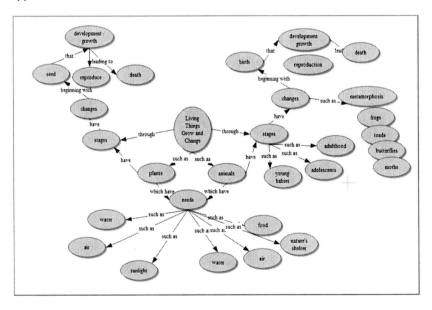

Figure 5-3. Grade 1 teacher concept map.

"When I think about teacher concept maps, I think about the difficulty it can be to start, but the power they have in helping me craft a unit."—Kari, SWH teacher.

The benchmark, big idea and teacher concept map are all essential to the process. They provide a foundation for the learning that will happen during the unit. Thus far, everything has been focused on the teacher. This approach is about making student's ideas public, so they have opportunities to challenge their own thinking and compare it to what others say. The only way to do that is to find out what they know.

FINDING OUT WHAT KIDS KNOW

Teachers approach this aspect of the SWH in many ways. Some are more comfortable with a traditional K-W-L chart while others support kids in developing a concept map. The concept map, in my opinion, gives the teacher more opportunity to see how kids see pieces connected. Whatever the strategy, a strong implementer will be able to talk about what kids know and don't know. They see it as an assessment that will help them make informed decisions on who needs what. Teachers beginning to use the approach may find out what kids know, but it can stop there. They aren't sure what to do with the information. Stronger implementers not only see it as a way to guide their instruction, but a way for students to concretely see how their ideas are changing.

Figure 5-4 is an example of a class concept map. Kids were asked to write down everything they knew in relation to their big idea. This included what parts of the plants and animals are used for survival. They were then asked to group them the best way they knew how. They labeled some of the groups' basic needs, survival techniques, and body parts. They used arrows and linking verbs to connect all the pieces. As you can see in the illustration, the teacher changed color of stickies to help

Figure 5-4. Class concept map.

kids see that they were gaining knowledge to add to the map. The students also asked if they could rearrange as they investigated their questions further and added pictures of examples they found of adaptations. The concept map was constantly changing and growing—a perfect reflection of how the students' learning was constantly changing and growing. The students could easily describe their class's beginning ideas. It was exciting and motivating to them to have their ideas valued (whether they were scientifically correct or not when first revealed).

As the professional development provider, I listen for what strategy a teacher is using to reveal student understanding, what information they gain from that strategy, what they will change in their instruction because of that information, and how they will use the strategy as the unit progresses. My coaching questions will hopefully help them strengthen the alignment of what they are doing instructionally with how students learn.

GENERATING QUESTIONS

Following the strategy to find out what kids' beginning ideas are, SWH teachers frequently have students generate questions. These questions are generated around the big idea which reflects the benchmark and will provide direction for the unit. Students can work with the questions in many ways. I've observed teachers that have asked their students to sort the questions into Need to Know, Good to Know and Fun to Know. Also, I have observed groups such as Researchable and Testable. Whatever the grouping, students in these classrooms are analyzing what questions will best help them learn more about the big idea.

Groupings and discussions can be extremely informative to the teacher. This is the type of information I would be listening and looking for as a professional developer. Does the teacher value student questions? Does the teacher look at student questions as a way for kids to negotiate their understanding? Does the opportunity provide information to the teacher on what kids know and don't know? Will the information impact their instructional decisions? Do kids own the questions or are they all the teachers? Is there a list of questions reflecting a high degree of involvement by the class or is the number limited? Are the questions used to guide follow-up investigations? Are there frequent opportunities for kids to interact with the questions both individually and in groups?

CLAIMS AND EVIDENCE

Generally teachers can predict what questions are going to lend themselves to rich conversations around students' claims and evidence. Kids are coached on how to design an investigation. Answering the beginning questions, what kind of data they will collect, how they will record the data and what the data says to them about their question? Students are then able to craft a claim based on evidence.

Many beginning teachers have trouble distinguishing between data and evidence. One analogy I share with them is that of a crime scene. Crime scene investigators will collect everything. Fingerprints, fibers, photos, even statements from people that may not have been involved, are collected. The detectives then analyze all the data to determine what evidence supports their guilty claim. Not everything becomes evidence—only the data that supports the claim. Teachers need to coach students in this same type of analysis—what data pieces help tell the "story" of their claim?

Beginning implementers often have students "share" their claims and evidence sometime allowing others to ask questions or even asking the questions themselves. This is often done as a presentation. It is often a monologue with no true debate of ideas. Strong SWH teachers recognize the power of a conversation. A rich claims and evidence conversation involves all kids. Its purpose is not to "prove someone wrong" but to further the group's learning. Students listen and question to understand. It is often passionate and lengthy. Alternative explanations are explored. Themes are uncovered. A teacher's role is to probe, question, and encourage participation. Teachers confident in this aspect of the approach will often use language such as, "What do you think?," "Who agrees/disagrees?," "Who can add to what was just said?" In this type of claims and evidence conversation the teacher takes a back seat—kids are talking to one another, not necessarily the teacher.

STUDENT TO STUDENT TALK

Student to student talk is another indicator of strong SWH implementation. This is a feature that is an obvious observation in classrooms. As I visit SWH classrooms, I sometimes see students sitting in rows and columns. More often, I see students around tables or their desks arranged in groups. This allows for either planned or unplanned negotiation opportunities. Strong SWH teachers understand the power of negotiations. People negotiate or learn, privately and publically. Negotiation takes place through reading, writing, speaking, listening, and viewing. Student to student talk is one way kids negotiate. Teachers that set up their classroom to support that type of negotiation are supporting that type of learning.

Student to student talk should take place during every component of the SWH approach. During my classroom visits I like to see kids talking as they examine their beginning ideas, generate questions, design experiments, collect data, craft claims and evidence, debate their ideas, reflect on their learning and even plan summary writing pieces. The amount of student to student talk should greatly outweigh the amount of teacher talk. Sometimes this is a struggle for teachers as they learn about this approach. It is often hard for us to "shush up and let them learn." Students need to work together to wrestle with the big idea and their own understanding of it. They should not be trying to guess what is in the head of the teacher. Student to student talk helps build that climate that every child's ideas are valued and should be made public.

To record what they knew about how weather changes, one first grade classroom worked in groups. As they recorded ideas about the seasons, the teacher listened and looked for what the kids knew (i.e. snow melts in the spring) and what they might not yet know or have incorrect understanding around (i.e. no ideas of changing temperature in the summer category). The conversations were exciting the students. People were listening to what they thought. The teacher wasn't trying to tell them if they were right or wrong. The power was in the conversation. Coming closer to

*Figure 5-5. Students work on a group negotiated understanding
of their most recent investigation.*

scientifically correct ideas could come later when they could challenge one another's ideas (Does it freeze everywhere in the winter?) and or as they consulted the experts (Who can we ask about snow?).

Kid to kid talk also allows for more students to be actively involved (See Figure 5-5). If the teacher is calling on one student at a time in a classroom, only one student is actively participating in the conversation. If a teacher asks students to talk at their table, more students are engaged. Telling kids to turn and talk to a partner can increase that number even further. Strong SWH implementers use varied and frequent strategies to increase the amount of student to student talk that happens in their classroom.

STUDENT REFLECTIONS

There should be many opportunities for students to reflect on their changing under-standing in an SWH classroom. Students should be adding and revising to the begin-ning concept map or KWL chart. Following every SWH investigation, students should be reflecting on how their beginning ideas are the same or different after having debated alternative explanations and consulting the experts. Every day in an SWH classroom can end with a journal entry on "How did today help me better understand the big idea?"

These reflections should be often, varied and on-going. SWH teachers know that having kids reflect on their changing ideas is a way for them to negotiate

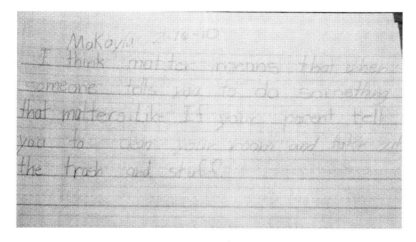

Figure 5-6. Student reflection on learning.

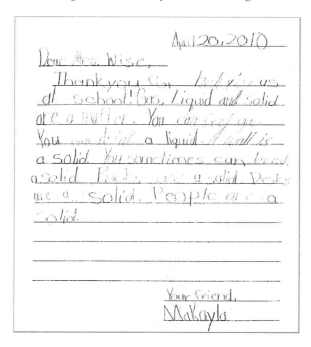

Figure 5-7. Student reflection on learning.

their understanding. It is also informative for the teacher. This child's journal entry (see Figure 5-6) shows that the student values cleaning her room and other chores, but doesn't understand the scientific meaning of matter. Again, it isn't a judgment—it is just data. This teacher should be able to talk to me about what additional learning opportunities she'll provide for Makayla to understand what matter is and how it relates to the class's big idea.

Another way for students to reflect on their own learning is for them to create a summary writing piece. The summary writing piece allows the student reflections on what they've learned, and summarize it in a way that shows new understanding. Students would use knowledge of purpose, audience, format in developing their writing piece. They would also use an effective writing process. When speaking to teachers I listen to how they value the summary writing piece, and the support they will provide for the writing process. The same student in Figure 5-6 wrote this summary writing piece in Figure 5-7. The teacher and Makayla were able to talk about how her ideas had changed from beginning to end.

LITERACY INTEGRATION

Literacy is foundational to the SWH approach. Students are involved in reading, writing, listening, viewing and speaking as they negotiate the big ideas of science. As a professional developer I am always looking for ways teachers are using literacy to promote negotiation of the concept, but also are they using the concept as an opportunity to learn more about literacy. In a recent classroom visit, a fifth grade teacher coached kids on how their study of generalizations might help them craft their claims. The students brainstormed a list of words authors use to begin a generalization. The teacher then coached the students to possibly use those words as they wrote their claim for their current investigation. One small group was struggling so the teacher pulled them aside to provide a short focused instructional piece to get them unstuck and on their way.

If this approach is about learning, why wouldn't we use science content to as additional opportunities for literacy use, assessment and instruction? I look for all three in SWH classrooms. One SWH teacher schedules her day by "learning zones" versus reading time, science time, etc. She has embraced a learning lens and knows that she can help kids become successful by an application of their literacy skills.

TEACHING AND LEARNING AS AN APPROACH

As I use a lens of learning while visiting classrooms, there should be ample evidence that a teacher has embraced teaching and learning as a part of their instruction. All the aspects described in this chapter should be used together in teaching a big idea— not as independent strategies.

The classroom should be student-centered. Student ideas and learning should be the center of attention. Student work should be displayed to represent their developing understanding around the big idea. The climate should be one of safety—where those ideas are valued and respected. The environment should be collaborative. Kid to kid talk should be frequent and encouraged. Reflections should be used to communicate learning. Assessments are seen as a way to gauge progress toward an understanding of the big idea and a way to plan additional learning opportunities. Teachers that embrace the SWH as an approach to learning are passionate about how each and every student can learn. One year into SWH training, we asked teachers to reflect on their beliefs. The following is one teacher's response:

As an SWH teacher, I believe....

- ONLY students are in charge of their learning
- Although I am frustrated a lot with SWH, I am better in my role as a teacher with the SWH
- Communication/language is an ESSENTIAL part of science (and everything else)
- To change pre-set frameworks, students must decide what they think they know is no longer adequate or enough
- NEGOTIATION is ESSENTIAL (self, peers, teacher, text, audience)
- Learning is more than memorizing and guessing what's in my head
- Learning is around the big ideas, NOT minute details, vocabulary, etc.
- Learning is about looking for AN answer, not THE ONE answer

These reflections are what excite me as a professional developer. I'm excited for the teacher who will get to witness the joy of true learning every day in her classroom. I'm excited for the students who finally feel like their voices are valued and they CAN learn and achieve. I'm especially excited for the future of our world. Each day, SWH teachers and students are proving that when student learning is the focus of the classroom, all things are possible.

Kim Wise
Green Hills Area Education Agency
Harlan, Iowa, USA

JOSHUA STEENHOEK, KARI PINGEL AND JILL PARSONS

6. THE POWER OF NEGOTIATION

Our interest in the Science Writing Heuristic came about as we were searching for methods to improve writing in our science classrooms. We were hoping to find answers on how we might connect the science writing process to our language arts curriculum. Our elementary school had committed several years to the study and integration of the 6+1 Writing Traits, and we wanted to continue down that path by looking for specific strategies that could help us produce better, nonfiction writers. We had absolutely no idea the training would become something more than just a workshop on writing, it would become an experience that would change the way we viewed teaching.

When we began our work with the Science Writing Heuristic trainers, we spent time looking at our unit overviews and reflecting on the progress of our students had made over the last several years. We were satisfied with the products our students were creating, and we felt truly confident that our students were getting a solid science education. Our lessons and projects were unique. Kids and parents were pleased with the engaging aspects of the units, and our students could certainly demonstrate highly acceptable performances on district and state science tests. We were content that our units matched effectively to our state core and the national science standards. So yes, we were pretty much congratulating ourselves on a job well done! However, it took a simple question to throw that sense of pride right out the window. We were asked, "Who is in charge of learning?"

After debating this strange notion that somehow our 5th grade students were in charge of their own learning, an uncomfortable series of questions got us buzzing back in our hotel room. If students are in charge of their own learning, then where the heck does that leave the teacher? If teachers are not in charge, then what is their role? How could a bunch of kids be in charge of learning? Have these trainers ever been in a real classroom?

It was a tough rest of the week, and we tried (to no avail) to defend what we had been doing to educate our students. As a group, we were resistant to change our practice, yet we had a nagging feeling our teaching practice might have to change in the fall. Yet, school started and so began our teaching. We started our science unit like we always had, but now we carefully decided to use the Science Writing Heuristic to compliment our science investigation. We videotaped our teaching and watched our practices. Each day as our team reflected on the lessons, we were able to see that our creative and unique ways of transferring information to the kids was just that, transferring of our knowledge to the kids. Very little learning was taking place. Even though we had the student heuristic as a guideline, we tried to make the process fit

B. Hand and L. Norton-Meier, (eds.), Voices from the Classroom: Elementary Teachers' Experience with Argument–Based Inquiry, 61–71.

into our unit plan. No matter how we tired to spin it, we were just finding hands-on ways to get our students to use a scientific protocol to memorize science information and expecting the students to deliver it back to us. It was not working, and we became extremely frustrated.

As we stumbled through the unit, our 5th grade team met more often to collaborate and discuss our progress (or lack of!) With consensus, we decided the best step we could take, was to regroup and focus on student negotiation. We agreed that we would avoid "Guess what's in my head?" questions, we would let the students lead the majority of the discussions, and we would not succumb to giving quick answers when the students turned to us for the "right" answers.

GETTING STARTED

It would be quite misleading if we claimed our students were suddenly transformed into self-led and productive negotiators. If anything, we found that our students would certainly talk, but they rarely listened to their peers. They could easily criticize claims made by others, but they could not follow up with why or suggest alternative claims/ evidence that were any better. The classroom discussion could die quickly with periods of complete silence, as the kids were waiting for us to lead. Quite clearly, our students did not know how to negotiate, because they had never been given the opportunity to do so. Our students not only needed multiple opportunities to compare their thinking with classroom peers, they needed time to compare it to science text and the larger learning community. We wanted our students to improve their communication skills, and we knew we had to get our students to hold each other accountable for their use of evidence. We began to see our role as "facilitator-leader" transform into classroom "manager." Our classroom environment was changing, and it demanded a shift into argument-based inquiry. Our curriculum had to change, and we realized our planning practices had to change, too.

With negotiation and language now being the center of how our students learn, our science planning has begun to look different. It is not that our old activities and units have completely disappeared, but now we structure our planning differently. Science "big ideas" drive the start of our units, not science content. A combination of student questions and our observation of student understanding about a particular big idea lead our daily lesson planning. We keep the collection of science activities/ investigations in our unit plan each year, but we are always prepared to provide a different activity, demonstration or investigation if the class discussion and questioning lead us down a slightly different path from the year before. No matter what direction the students follow, all paths are carefully designed to lead back to the big idea. Looking at planning with a big idea in mind has changed our view of what parts of our curriculum are valuable. It has naturally forced our 5th grade science teachers to have a better understanding of the science we teach. As our understanding improves, our negotiation of WHY we do what we do each day becomes rich, and some days even more complex!

Our planning process is not linear, but we feel we have a reliable system that currently works for us. The first step we take is to access the state standards and determine whether our units align and make sure we do not have gaps between the grade levels above and below us. Then, as a group of three teachers, we create a concept map that illustrates our own understanding of the unit topic. From there, we identify what our essential questions and concepts for fifth graders will be based on our framework of understanding and state standards. With all of this in mind, we create one simplistic statement that captures the 'big idea' of the entire unit. For example, the big idea for our forces and motion unit is forces affect motion. The key to remember about creating your big idea is that it must be appropriate for your grade level, written in short, simple, student friendly language, and be broad enough to capture all of the essential learning from the unit but small enough to be understood at various levels. After we have our big idea, we go back to all of the activities and projects that we do already and start to link them where they match to the essential learning we identified in our concept framework. Where there are gaps, we begin to discuss and seek out possible activities, readings, and experiences the students would need or want in order to help answer their questions. Once we have the unit organized and set-up, we examine ideas to start the unit and plan for various assessments depending on the direction of the class. The key to assessment is each assessment has to tie back to the students' understanding of the big idea.

The Science Writing Heuristic has revolutionized our forces in motion unit. Outlining and planning a unit as a teacher is difficult, but it is not nearly as nerve-racking as standing in front of a classroom full of kids and actually doing something with it. When teachers go back to the fundamentals of what students know and work to move forward to an improved understanding, it only seems logical to start with their beginning understanding.

We begin by finding an activity that will elicit what the students know. This activity must be directly tied to the personality of your class. One year we had a class that was decidedly linear and chose to use a concept map to organize their beginning ideas due to their nature of being visual and structural in the framework of their knowledge. Another year, we had a class that was more creative and abstract. This group of students chose to write and illustrate their beginning ideas in picture notes. Though both of these ways are drastically different, the teacher gained the information they were looking for.

Regardless of how you begin it is essential to choose the strategy that is most comfortable for the students so that you get the most out of the experience. The information we gather from students' beginning ideas is used in two basic ways: 1) to identify students' scientifically incorrect understandings and 2) to have an idea of which activities would be redundant to proceed with, based on the students' correct understanding, and which ones would be beneficial to do based on their missing framework. Classroom time is too precious to waste on concepts that students already understand.

Once students have had the opportunity to share their beginning thinking, they naturally start asking questions based on other's ideas and others' critique of their ideas. We make those questions public by recording them in the classroom in one of two categories: testable or researchable. During this process, the students begin to see the framework of the questions and then begin to sequence them into a logical order. When the students have finally prioritized their list of questions, the teacher decides what activity (from the list created on the unit plan) might best help them answer their question and resolve any misunderstandings. Ample time will be provided for each activity so that the students can process their new understanding of the big idea. Purposefully planning each investigation with the students will help them fully answer their questions and address their scientifically inaccurate thinking.

Even though sometimes you might have had a good activity and powerful negotiation, some students will move forward in their understanding, but others will still have rooted misunderstandings they are not ready/unwilling to let go. This is where the continued exposure will not only push the understanding of some students, but also allow others to shift their thinking for the first time.

Throughout this whole process, as well as at the end, students need to be more metacognitive with their thinking. Often we focus on the reflection piece by merely asking the students to think about how their ideas have changed from the beginning of the unit to now. While that is good, we also need to keep asking them to reflect on the questions. "How did this activity help me better understand the big idea?" What do I currently understand about the big idea?" "What questions do I still have about the big idea?" These questions must be asked frequently throughout the entire unit. The questions may seem simplistic, but these questions are essential in the assessment of each child's learning.

As teachers, we need to change our focus from the idea that students must know specific pieces of content, to the idea that they must have an understanding of a concept. So how do we actually know when our students understand a concept? How do they ever learn the content? Assessment continues to plague our use of SWH. When we finally let go of using letter grades and moved more toward formative assessment of the essential things that scientists must do (investigation, negotiation, engagement, literacy, concept understanding), the students started to have more purpose for what they were doing in class and assessment became easier. Students were no longer afraid to be wrong and not only began to seek further understanding of science concepts and content, but also wanted to improve their ability to think critically as a scientist. Giving students a specific learning target(s) for the day, focuses the students on where and how to improve their skills and concept understanding. When most students are fully able to answer the majority of their questions and use those answers to better explain their new understanding of the big idea, you know that you are able to move on to the next unit. Traditionally, teachers have measured whether they can move on by student mastery of individual pieces of content. However, our focus now centers on student understanding of the big idea. If we are continually asking students to explain what they know about the big idea, they will instinctively pick up the essential pieces of content as they broaden this understanding of the concept, because the content has actually become relevant.

Food for Thought: If you have 20 minutes left in class and your lesson is completed, use the time for another subject. Do not force the learning, rather, be purposeful with your management.

WHAT CAN YOU EXPECT FROM A 5TH GRADER

The changes that happen for students from the beginning of 5th grade to the end of the year in 5th grade became apparent when we started using the SWH approach.

Now, what our students are capable of doing by the end of the year is remarkable. This happened because we let THEM push their own learning and think for themselves.

All teachers want their students to be engaged in their classrooms and often use strategies and activities/projects to accomplish that engagement. Students become disconnected and do not have an interest because it is not following their questions. Switching the roles and using the students' questions to direct your activities gives them a sense of ownership and increases their engagement. After the opening activity, students begin to desire answers to the questions they do not know. It has taken us awhile, but we finally figured out that you would get poor quality questions if you let kids just randomly generate questions about what they want to know. There does have to be purpose in their questions. Our quality questions changed when we made the rule that all questions must directly relate back to the big idea. After some practice and modeling, the students will begin to hold each other accountable for the questions they ask by challenging each question they feel may be unrelated: "How does that help us learn about the big idea?" If an adequate answer can not be agreed upon, the question is put into the "nice to know" pile. There also continues to be a small group of students who immediately claim to know the answer to questions posed by the class. However, once they are challenged to explain how it is they know the answer to that question, they begin to back pedal. A rule of thumb is that you do not actually know what you can not explain.

Once the list of questions is created and students decide their unit focus, they implement the appropriate activity from your planning. It is important to remember that just because an activity has been planned, it does not have to be used. The activities selected should be chosen based on the students' background knowledge and need for understanding of the big idea. The activities do not always have to be teacher led. Sometimes students can devise their own tests by simply providing materials and allowing them an opportunity to play.

For example, near the beginning of the unit, we put out small catapult guns and various items to be launched. Students immediately picked them up and started trying things. Unconsciously they began asking questions and testing variables. After a few minutes, students came back together to discuss different variables that could be tested with the catapult guns. As students list possible variables to test on the board, they also have to pose it in the form of a question that can be linked back to one of the big idea questions. From there, they can begin to divide up the questions among groups, devise a plan to test their variable and conduct the test.

This process does not happen in an instant. Throughout the year, students have to learn through trial and error, how to conceptually devise a test before they can actually write it out in steps. At the 5th grade level, students are comfortable acting out their test without being precise with their variables. While acting out their test, they are looking for common relationships for what is happening before they begin to break it down into a step-by-step procedure. Once they feel like they can explain their test and how they are controlling the variables, they go public and share with the class to gain approval before actually conducting the test. The approval becomes essential for all students because they are relying on the data of other groups to weave into their own claim and evidence. When the class has given its approval, the students begin to conduct their tests and record their data.

After the students have completed their tests, they move into the analysis of their data. Something simple can become so complicated when done by a 5th grader. Early in the year, students learn how to create charts, generate graphs, and look for trend lines. The interpretation of graphs or looking at trend lines helps students to keep their focus on one specific piece of data but rather look at the whole picture. Students move from an analysis such as "the lightest one went the farthest" to "the lighter the object, the farther it will travel." Then, the higher order thinking actually begins. The students are required to synthesize a statement that answers why their analysis happened. That statement or claim should also answer or clarify one or more of their beginning questions.

HOW DO YOU GET THERE

We have found that encouraging the students to write down all of their data (observations, information that they have read, previous experiences, background knowledge) helps them to see the bigger picture. Students begin to sketch out their ideas and support what has happened by pulling in the relevant pieces of data. Once the students have an understanding of what happened, they condense it into their claim. Then they weave their evidence together by finding supporting pieces of information to explain how and why that claim is true. This claim should be a clear statement that answers the beginning question and shows a connection to the big idea. At this point, this first version of their claim and evidence has only been negotiated by themselves and their small group, but it is now ready to go public for further scientific critique.

At the beginning of the year, our 5th grade students are weak in their negotiation skills because they have never been afforded the opportunity to challenge others' ideas or have their ideas challenged by others.

Since our students have not had any previous experience with SWH, they enter into our classrooms still seeking confirmation from peers and the teacher. They sit at their desks and look to us expecting us to tell them what they want/need to know. As the silence continues, the students who have been labeled "smart" will offer ideas, but even when incorrect, others will not challenge them. So, as the teacher, we start challenging those students regardless if they are scientifically correct or not and that is where disequilibrium begins creating an even playing field. It is no longer satisfactory for the smart kids to answer the questions so that they can be confirmed and the whole class moves on. Now, all voices are equally valuable to the discussion. Oddly enough, at the beginning of the year, students who are the quietest in the classroom can come up with some of the best ideas. Their increased confidence appears to be due to no longer being told they are incorrect. Now that all students have become equals to each other, the teacher has the opportunity to learn and negotiate with them.

The teacher's role in negotiation is actually quite complicated. Not only does the teacher need to be focused on the classroom dynamics, or making sure that there is respectful dialogue and students are focused on the idea not the person, but they also have to be listening all the time to make sure students are held accountable for what they say. It is easy for a student to suggest something or state a piece of knowledge that they have heard but not actually have to back it up with evidence. When the students miss the opportunity to challenge each other, the teacher needs to step in and expose that lack of evidence. However, by the end of the year, the teacher's role is minimal, because students assume those two major roles due to the modeling and space we have provided.

For example, in a previously completed unit, our students publicly negotiated their claims. One group in particular shared their claim "objects with less mass go further than objects with more mass". Initially, most students nodded in agreement, but as the students started to think about the claim, you could see them start to question its accuracy. Finally, one group asked them which they could throw farther, a water balloon filled with air or a balloon filled with water?

Group 1 response: "Duh, a water balloon!"

Student 1 response: "But you said lighter objects should go further with the same force, so shouldn't the balloon filled with air go further?"

Student 2 response: "I agree that in your test, lighter objects went further, but that claim doesn't always work because you can throw a water balloon with water farther."

Group 2 response: "In our test, we found there was a relationship between force and mass. Our claim is objects resist change. Objects that are lighter are easier to move and objects that are heavier take more effort to move."

Group 1 response: "What does that have to do with us launching?"

Group 2 response: "Well, it is important because your heavier object took more of the catapults force to move and the lighter object took less to move."

Student 2 response: "Well shouldn't the air water balloon go really far if that is true because it is really light and your force should move it really easy."

Group 2 response: "Well, it does take less force to move, but it also takes less force to stop. So, the air balloon is thrown really easily, but the air friction around it also slowed it down very fast. The water balloon took more force to throw, but also fought through the air friction before it was pulled back to Earth."

At this point in time, the group moved from thinking their claim was 100% accurate to having to go back and rethink their results.

During this time, the teachers questioned students who were not speaking up and managed volume and tone. The rest was guided and organized by the students. We took notes on what students said, who said what, how students supported their thinking, and ideas on what to do if the inaccurate claim persisted. After a few more rounds of this public negotiation, the students reached a point where they were comfortable with their claims and evidence, and how it advanced their understanding of the big idea, force affects motion. As 5th graders, they recognized the importance of what other experts in the field have to say about their topic. The students do not compare with the experts just to compare and practice researching, it is a time for their ideas can be strengthened, solidified, or renegotiated if inaccurate thinking is found.

Could we have just given them readings and discussed them? Could we have told them how force affects mass ($f=ma$)? Had them repeat it back to us? Asked questions and waited for right answers? Yes, but instead, students recognized that they are in charge of their learning. They made a claim. Others disagreed. It took the experience of being comfortable enough to speak up and disagree, as well as actually seeing a different scenario where their claim did not work, for students to begin to make a change in thinking. The students continued to work on their claim based on further negotiations in the room and eventually got to a scientifically accurate claim that the class could agree on, but it took dissonance, experience…learning!

HOW TECHNOLOGY HELPS

Technology has typically played a supporting role in our science classrooms. We use computers to research questions or find information that is not readily available in the classroom. Our students use different software programs to collect and organize data that they can more easily analyze from their investigations, and we have used simulation software to enhance science experiments or demonstrations that can be difficult to conduct in our classrooms. However, what we have found is that many of our students use technology somewhat differently outside the classroom walls. They are certainly accessing and absorbing the explosion of information that is readily available to them on the Internet (whether valid or not). However, they are also texting, chatting and emailing with their peers, which is informally writing to communicate. How could we take our students' motivation to collaborate electronically, and enhance their written communication in science? Let us introduce you to Moodle.

Moodle is an open source, on-line learning management system that allows a user to create on-line science courses. Teachers can build assignments, post web-links, attach files and even create assessments that can be graded by the software. There are a variety of activity modules that allow teachers to set up wikis, forums and databases.

Because our science students primarily communicate with their peers through verbal discussion, we have used Moodle's collaboration module to create collaborative science forums. We are constantly looking to capture the great conversations that take place around the SWH argument structures and transfer them into effective written forms of communication. These forums provide our students with a platform to start and continue science classroom discussions by sharing their claims with an authentic audience.

Requiring our students to communicate their scientific conclusions from an SWH science investigation is the "concrete evidence" we collect from our students that demonstrate the critical thinking they are able to do. When our students are given multiple writing opportunities to express thoughts and support those thoughts with evidence, they begin to understand the importance of the language they need to use to express those ideas. However, getting students to write claims and support those claims with solid evidence and clear explanation, is a process that requires time, modeling, and lots of practice! We believe the writing of claims and evidence may be the most difficult part of the science process for our students, and we are continually looking to assist our students in writing to explain. Using Moodle is one way we can utilize technology to motivate our students to write, and also teach them the 21st Century skills of collaborating, communicating and productively contributing to the world of information.

When our students use a Moodle forum to post their claims and evidence, they must write to a critical and diverse audience. Moodle allows 200 of our fifth graders to collaborate and discuss their science investigations. A student discussion is not just limited to a child's homeroom class. Instead, they can discuss ideas across multiple classrooms or other grade spans. Creating this type of writing environment demands students not only prepare an organized and well-written piece of writing, but they must think critically to respond when their evidence or explanations are challenged. Our students must now be accountable to others for their written claims, and they must be prepared to support whatever they post to the forum.

Writing claims with supporting evidence consumes much or our student's class-room time. In addition to the time students need to write, their writing requires some form of response from others to assess whether or not they are expressing themselves clearly and effectively. This editing, discussion, and revision process, too, can take precious days of classroom time. We have found that our Moodle forums can expedite the time it takes for students to get the immediate feedback they want and need. When students become accountable for posting their claims and evidence, and are also required to give effective feedback (this must be modeled and learned, as well) it can significantly reduce the amount of time it takes in class, and can be continued publicly without everyone being present.

We have observed many of our students posting discussion threads on the science forums well after school hours. We had a young lady create a post that read: "Okay, I can not talk about rocket nose cones anymore because my mom says I have to quit "talking" on Moodle. I have to brush my teeth and get ready for bed!" Really, how does an educator get kids to continue discussing and problem solving when they are getting their PJ's on? Answer, an innovative technology and an environment that can support how students learn. Not only will your confident and articulate students spend time writing on Moodle, but you may be pleasantly surprised at how they may not dominate the discussion threads like one might expect. Much to our surprise, we have witnessed reluctant speakers and shy students become active leaders in scientific argument when given this type of writing forum. Moodle provides each child with a password-protected, teacher monitored, on-line learning community where he/she can feel safe expressing ideas. Our students can work from home to respond and collaborate at their own pace without the pressures of limited class time, verbally dominant peers, and intimidating large groups.

As teachers, we can take these nightly discussion threads and weave them into classroom conversations the next day. These threads can be used to stimulate new questions and enhance claims and evidence through the common themes and problems students are encountering throughout all of the 5th grade science classes. The dis-cussions can help a student in one class affirm that his investigation results and claims are supported by others when perhaps the majority of his class is in disagreement.

As our students begin to ask more complex questions, seek answers to those questions, think critically about their results, and compare their conclusions with others in the scientific community, we begin to better understand the importance of information, communication and technology literacy. Our state core standards emphasize the need for districts to begin addressing how they are preparing students to be equipped with 21st Century skills; we feel an arguments-based science classroom provides the perfect opportunity for students to hone these skills. We know every one of our students has thoughts and ideas to contribute, and Moodle gives students that chance. Our science students are continuing to take part in scientific arguments in their world, on their time, because the technology seamlessly fits into their lives outside of school. This is exactly what we want our students to understand about learning. It does not end when they walk out the school doors.

REFLECTION

Throughout the entire process of trying to better understand an argument-based approach to teaching inquiry, we continue to realize that there are always new questions that arise, and we are constantly challenged with unique situations. Such is the nature of teaching science. We do, however, see our students developing critical thinking skills that move them to ask fantastic questions, but the answers to those questions cannot always be found through our classroom investigations or discussions. This continues to be a challenge, yet a constant reminder, that we as teachers are not the "holders of the answers." It is this pursuit of learning that drives our inquiry-based classrooms.

Inquiry has transferred into our math classrooms as well, because our students are no longer complacent with the simple transfer of knowledge. Instead of telling students how to divide or how to make equivalent fractions, our students now tackle carefully planned questions/problems that allow for open-ended learning opportunities that get the students figuring out how and why. Letting students explore and discuss the variety of ways math can be understood and calculated together, begins to calm the anxiety that can result from students who cannot learn the "book rules" or process math quickly. It also allows for stronger math students to communicate what they know and why they know it, instead of math being a series of learned rules with little understanding of why those rules work.

A rich discussion will ensue if children become used to an environment that encourages and expects students to discuss, explain, and concretely represent their thinking. Kids will generate a variety of ways to solve, represent, and explain their solutions much better than we ever could hope. What's better? The discussion around the math problem engages more students productively than any lecture or activity could. When students begin to realize that their thinking and connections are valued and needed (whether right or wrong) to help the rest of us understand mathematics, they want to analyze other's ideas because they own the learning. It is this slight change in the way teachers view how students learn and how they "deliver" other content areas that will improve complex thinking.

We started this journey trying to improve writing. Our students are undeniably writing more than we had ever anticipated they could, but we are not quite satisfied that we have developed writers that can write high quality claims, evidence, or explanations. Our first year focused on what is teaching and what is learning and trying to figure out our role in management with the students. We knew we were not going to get anywhere until we figured that out. Once we struggled through it, we spent the next 2 years exploring the different facets of negotiation. Now, we are seeing this impressive critical thinking and learning is happening in our classroom, but we are struggling with how to authentically assess it. We find ourselves trying to assess behavior (which is objective), trying to assess negotiation (which is the student's learning and who am I to judge their learning - based on different academic levels, attitude, personality, and effort), and trying to assess things that have never been asked of them before. We are now assessing the abstract rather than the concrete, and it is not what we are used to assessing. However, as a team we have seen an immense change in our science classrooms. We are getting more out of students than ever before, because we actually let them decide and show what they are capable of doing, rather than limiting them by our own agenda. So, we will continue to seek and try these new assessments in order to push our students further in their science learning than ever before.

Joshua Steenhoek, Kari Pingel and Jill Parsons
Pella Community Schools
Pella, Iowa, USA

JULIE SANDER

7. IMPLEMENTING SCIENCE CONVERSATIONS WITH YOUNG LEARNERS

"Mrs. Sander! Mrs. Sander! Mrs. Sander!" Students rush up to me excited and ready to share. Teaching kindergarten and first grade students definitely has its perks and challenges. K-1 students are highly energetic, eager to participate, and most are enthusiastic about school and learning new information. The skills and concepts learned in these formative years combined with the application of this knowledge are imperative to the students' future successes. Understanding science concepts and learning through inquiry teaching are integral parts of this process. It is my goal to ensure my young learners are both learning and retaining scientific concepts. Using the Science Writing Heuristic approach in my classroom enhances these learning opportunities.

The Science Writing Heuristic approach embodies many of my personal teaching and learning goals. The SWH promotes student-centered learning, engages students in conversations. SWH also encourages students to ask questions, write claims with supporting evidence, negotiate ideas and disagreements, conduct experiments, and have fun with science. The SWH classroom has "students" at the forefront of both learning and instruction. Stepping back and allowing students to control the learning process, has made my teaching life *easier* and more *efficient*. The transition from the traditional teaching approach in science, using textbooks as the primary resource and implementing "skill and drill" lessons, to the SWH approach can be awkward and difficult, but with a little effort, it can be, and should be, done. This evolution in the classroom supports the common saying; *teach smarter, not harder.*

I find the traditional teaching approach to science is limiting for the teacher and students. The use of rigid lesson plans and student textbooks as the primary learning resource may conflict with students' learning styles. The use of the SWH approach has increased flexibility in my classroom; how students advance through lessons and determine claims has significantly expanded. The SWH approach encourages students to use a variety of resources including: contacting professionals in the specific area of study, using various media materials, and partaking in field trips, generate assorted experiments, and use inventive methods of presenting learned information such as poster presentations, reader's theatre scripts, poetry, dioramas. I encourage this creativity with all students in the classroom, reaching out to individual learning styles and personalities. With the increased student control in curriculum decisions, the SWH approach also promotes metacognition, thinking about thinking; encouraging students' self-reflection and higher level thinking process. My favorite transformation in the classroom is the students increased motivation to learn new things, ask more questions,

B. Hand and L. Norton-Meier, (eds.), Voices from the Classroom: Elementary Teachers'
Experience with Argument–Based Inquiry, 73–86.

and their determination to find the answers without relying on teacher approval; achieving the ultimate goal of graduating my classroom with a desire to learn more through self-directed learning methods.

The biggest challenge with my transition from the traditional teaching approach of "teacher led instruction" to "student led instruction" was increasing, encouraging, and allowing the young learners' *voices* to shine through this student-centered learning approach. Reflecting on the SWH methods and personal teaching/learning goals, encouraged me to explore "science conversations". Implementing these group discussions in the classroom helped me accomplish teaching objectives and strengthen learning opportunities for individual students and the classroom community. Soon I heard, "Mrs. Sander! Mrs. Sander! I have something to share at the science circle!"

HOW IT ALL BEGAN

As a new teacher to the school district, I reviewed the curriculum materials provided for my classroom. It was among these materials that I discovered a binder complete with grade level science units, articles for reflective science practices, detailed lesson plans and activities for teaching science in the classroom. This brief introduction of the science curriculum and the district's outlined Science Writing Heuristics units sparked my interest. Many of Science Writing Heuristics practices paralleled my own teaching practices and student goals; encouraging self-directed learning, teaching science concepts in an early childhood classroom, and using inquiry as a "driving force". Implementing the existing SWH units allowed me to "test the waters" and by the end of the school year, I had joined the SWH team!

The first SWH workshop that I attended in the summer inspired and encouraged teachers to allow students to control their learning and lead teacher instruction. Allowing 5–6 year olds to "control the classroom" was a scary idea. Initializing this classroom transformation required me to understand the curriculum, assessment standards, and available resources to pave the road teaching SWH in my classroom. Stepping into the classroom, I began this teaching style shift by asking students more questions; "*How* should we determine if all metal sinks when placed in water? *Why* does the wood pencil sink in water, but the wood block float in water?" Asking "why" after a student response is an excellent strategy to encourage higher-level thinking; the requirement of students to reflect on their thinking process. For example, a student may comment, "Snakes are cool". A teacher could reply, "*Why* are they cool?" Asking more questions, avoiding the desire to "give answers", increasing "wait time" (the time given after a question is asked by a teacher and an additional comment made by that teacher), and allowing students to make decisions during experiments encouraged me to *listen* to student voices; all strategies encouraged when using the SWH approach. The success was evident in my first teaching experiences using SWH, and I wanted to maximize these positive learning experiences. The students responded with enthusiasm and an eagerness to participate. Initially, this conversion was intimidating, but all instruction can be tailored to individual and classroom needs. Lesson plans can be modified and adjusted to reflect the SWH approach. "Diving in" is the best approach.

GETTING STARTED USING SWH IN THE CLASSROOM

In my kindergarten classroom, I generally teach the first SWH unit one or two months into the school year. The first few weeks of school, my kindergarten classroom is consumed with teaching daily routines, schedules, and following basic rules. I found first graders are ready for the first SWH unit a bit sooner, as early as the first month of classes. In both grades, I use the first unit to focus on the process of the Science Writing Heuristics approach. The initial activities prepare young students by discussing investigation, inquiry, organizing thoughts and making connections using concept maps, writing about science ideas, and sharing/learning with others (see Figure 1).

In Figure 7-1, I share a variety of activities used in the initial SWH unit for kindergarten and First Grade. The first item displayed (and labeled as "a") is a kindergarten and first grade concept map titled, "I am a scientist." This concept map remains on the wall for the entire school year. Students repeat actions (Thinking-point to brain; Observation-point to eyes; Questioning- put hand in front of mouth and open; Experiment-rub hands together) when asked, "What is a scientist?" The second item displayed is labeled (b) and represents a kindergarten gobstopper activity.

Question	Yes	No
Do you like cookies?		
Do you like chocolate milk?		
Do you wear pink chapstick?		
Do you like chocolate?		
Were you in our building during our recess on Monday?		

Figure 7-1. Activities used for an initial SWH unit for kindergarten and first grade students.

Kindergarten students observe, discuss, and discover the effects of gobstoppers when placed in a cup of water. Finally, the third item in the figure labeled with a (c) shows an activity that we did called "Who Stole the Cookies from the Cookie Jar." This is the question sheet from the initial SWH unit first grade in which students investigated "Who stole the Cookies from the Cookie Jar?" Students provided these questions to "suspected" faculty members at our school.

These initial activities provide a foundation to the science curriculum in my classroom and students receive repeated practice throughout the school year. The formal process of investigation, writing claims, organizing thoughts, and building concept maps are learning practices repeated throughout the entire school year for my K-1 students. Using the SWH approach provides opportunities for students to learn these skills and practice our foundational skills of reading, writing, questioning, and applying basic conceptual knowledge, avoiding the traditional approach of rote memorization, lectures, and inflexible lesson plans. Since the conversion of using the SWH approach in the classroom, my students will cheer when I say, "Let's begin science".

An important area of focus in my K-1 classroom is enhancing students' writing skills. The SWH approach recognizes this fundamental skill and encourages writing in the classroom. This reinforces concepts and develops the student's writing abilities. Many of the students' writing skills are emerging, and I regularly modify lesson plans or activities for individual students and our classroom community. At the beginning of kindergarten, students often express their ideas using pictures and one-word captions. The construction of concept maps represents pictures or 3-D objects, and the teacher frequently serves as the "scribe". As the school year progresses, kindergarten students practice writing one sentence for their claims and writing several words for their picture captions. First Grade students learn to write multiple sentences for their science claims, share detailed observations in their science journals, and also assist the teacher with writing words on concept maps. The writing pieces and science journals used in the classroom are an ideal representation of student growth over the course of the school year. Students take considerable pride in their hard work and efforts symbolized in their science journals for each unit; decorating the journal covers, participating in daily writing entries, and carefully drawing pictures throughout their collective pieces. I also use the science journals as an additional example of student abilities and cumulative growth at spring conferences. The parents also appreciate the informative demonstration!

As stated earlier, using SWH methods in the classroom expands creativity and flexibility. There are endless possibilities writing in an SWH classroom! My kindergarten students wrote a song "We Need Trees" with a musician. My first grade students wrote pen-pal letters and acrostic poems. Kindergarten students identified how different food groups help our bodies grow by labeling personal outlines drawn on butcher paper. One student drew and labeled a carrot pointing to his eyes. Students are expanding their ideas and applying their skills using a variety of methods.

In Figure 7-2, I share several examples of concept maps used in kindergarten and first grade classroom. The first is a generic concept map used in the K-1 classroom. When creating concept maps, I assist with writing words as they share ideas.

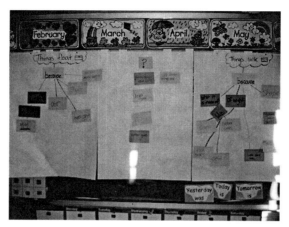

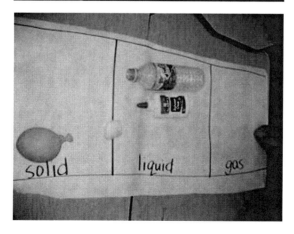

Figure 7-2. Examples of concept maps used in kindergarten and first grade classrooms.

Students can post the sticky notes on our concept maps and make connections. The different colored sticky notes represent different days; a new day or update of information receives a different color. Students assist with placing the sticky notes on the map, connecting the lines, and adding the linking words. The second concept map displayed in Figure 7-2 is a concept map created in a kindergarten classroom during the unit, "What is Fall?" Kindergarten students used the school district's digital cameras to capture images of fall. Finally, a 3-D concept map for our unit on matter created by first grade students prior to the unit is also displayed in Figure 7-2. Small groups of students sorted random objects in a bucket onto a blank concept map. Pictures were taken and enlarged for initial small group concept maps.

IMPLEMENTING SCIENCE CONVERSATIONS...

To embrace the SWH teaching approach, I needed to identify the students' current level of comprehension, encourage self-directed learning, and receive guidance on future lesson plans. I wanted to implement science conversations before, during, and after science activities to help reinforce ideas, develop discussion skills, encourage student-led learning, increase motivation, and assist the teacher with planning future lessons. I wanted to amplify my young learners' *voices* in the classroom and also lead daily instruction. Somehow, I needed to utilize *successful* science conversations with a classroom of 20 kindergarten or 20 first grade students, with only myself for damage control.

Eager to attempt student-led discussions, I reminded students of our friendly voices, listening to others, taking turns talking, sharing ideas, and directed the students to "share with each other without raising their hands". This initial attempt was a disaster. After my verbal prompt, students began talking all at once and steadily increasing the volumes in their voices; each student looking directly at me. This is not what I had envisioned.

I began brainstorming ways to improve these science conversations and collaborated with Sara Nelson (a graduate student working with the SWH team). We reviewed Gallas's (1995) work on "Science Talks" and *Questions, Claims, and Evidence* (Norton-Meier, et al. 2008). This provided us with an initial guidance. Both books described how discussions can assist learners in enhancing communication skills and their capacity to contribute and defend their ideas in science.

Understanding our goals with science conversations, the development of an early childhood learner, and embracing the Science Writing Heuristics approach, our plan began to form. Sharing voices with 19+ students has proven to be a difficult task in an early childhood classroom; taking turns, listening respectfully, defending ideas, and conversing with *each other* (not the teacher) are essential skills in this process. Using a tangible object as a reminder with some guiding "rules" may help develop these skills. A squishy, rubbery ball was the determining factor on the speaker. Students could "toss it around" and practice student-to-student dialogue. For the subsequent science conversation, I presented some new guidelines:
– You (students) are the teachers. My job is to write down all of your ideas on sticky notes.

- If you (students) are holding the ball, you may share your ideas. I will write down your ideas, and then you must say a classmate's name before you pass the ball to them (this prevents several children jumping in the middle of the circle and fighting over the object).
- Sometimes, I may ask you (students) to raise your hands if you have not shared any ideas. Then the speaker will pass the ball to a new person.
- If you (students) do not think someone is saying the right thing or you disagree, you may use your friendly voice and share your idea. It is exciting to have different ideas and share them.

Wow! This science conversation was a remarkable difference. The students understood the guidelines quickly, were eager to share, and I could hear and understand their science ideas. Sitting outside the students' science circle, I wrote down their shared ideas using a pad of sticky notes. As students eagerly shared their knowledge on "What is Fall?", I would write their thoughts using 1–3 words on a sticky note, and I continued this throughout the science conversation. I wrote down each student's idea; I wanted to send the message to my emerging literacy learners that *all ideas are* respected. Using a tangible object provided students with a concrete reminder on taking turns and listening to others. At the kindergarten level, I used this ball for most of the units. In first grade, I prefer to try Science Conversations without the tangible object as the year progresses, to encourage a more natural child-to-child dialogue.

Organizing a science conversation prior to all activities in a SWH unit has proved beneficial in my lesson planning. These science conversations provide teachers with students' background information, misconceptions, new ideas, and possible strengths. One student may share, "My dad is a plant scientist" or "I make kites with my grandpa". I enjoy listening to the direction of the conversation, as it informs me of future lesson plans. Our initial science conversation for "sink and float" brought an engaging (and long) disagreement about Barbie dolls "sinking" or "floating". After writing down "Barbie" on a post-it note, a student placed it under our "?" section on the concept map for later investigation. The students (and teacher) often investigate many student disagreements throughout an SWH unit. These investigations ensures content understanding and also embraces the ultimate goals of SWH; self-directed learning, inquiry, investigation, negotiating and defending ideas, and writing claims with supportive evidence. Students demonstrate a keen interest in these inquiries and control the process of investigation.

Throughout our sink and float unit, we tested many objects of varying sizes, shapes, and materials to determine the ultimate question of this specific classroom discussion, "What happens when a Barbie is placed in water; does the Barbie sink to the bottom, or does it float to the top of the water?" do Barbies sink or float when placed in water. After one week of experiments, making claims, reading books, implementing numerous science conversations, and writing our conclusions; we studied the Barbie doll's shape, size, and materials to state/write our final claims. The answer to our ultimate question concluded that Barbie's head floated and the Barbie's body sank. Student-led experiments are motivating, entertaining, and informative!

The "Barbie disagreement" stimulated students to ask more questions and investigate the "answer". Disagreements occur often throughout science units and science conversations, and teacher encouragement is necessary! We discuss our "friendly voices" frequently during our science block (and other daily activities). Teacher observations of student respect to other's ideas, particularly during our science block, enrich this experience. During our science block teacher reminders are not always sufficient, and these students are sent to his or her desk for "not being a good scientist". "Listening is part of being a good scientist"; I remind the students. In my personal experiences, students do not want to "miss out" during science, and I rarely need to use this method. Teaching with the SWH approach in my classroom has also encouraged and enhanced classroom management!

HOW SCIENCE CONVERSATIONS ENCOURAGE PARTICIPATION

Using science conversations in my classroom has encouraged all students to share ideas. Encouraging participation and building my classroom community is a top priority throughout the school day and school year. During our science block, this includes sharing and defending ideas (with respect). To hear all student voices, would open my ears and eyes to new possibilities. Creating lesson plans and activities adapted to the needs of my classroom, results in effective teaching practices. Students who share disagreements have provided new opportunities of "teachable moments".

For example, our initial science conversation during our sponges unit, a disagreement erupted among students:

> "A quiet student, Tommy, shared, "Sponges are found in the ocean." Other students replied, "No they are not." Tommy claimed again, "Yes they are, they are found in the ocean." More students agreed that sponges are *not* found in the ocean. Recognizing Tommy's frustration, I intervened and said, "Let's put a question mark on the concept map next to this idea, and we will search for the answer right away."

> The following day, we read the book *Sponges Are Skeletons* (1993) by Barbara Juster Esbensen. It was a joy to see the proud look on Tommy's face when students discovered that natural sponges *are* indeed found in the ocean". (Sander & Nelson, 2009, p. 44–45)

We immediately updated the concept map removing the sticky note "sponges are alive" from the "?" board and included this confirmed idea under our initial heading, "Sponges". Students assisted with connecting our big idea to this sticky note using a black marker and taping a connecting word to our concept map. In my classroom, science conversations have proven an excellent approach to reduce misconceptions, increase participation, and allow students to control their learning.

BUILDING CONCEPT MAPS USING SCIENCE CONVERSATIONS

In my classroom, the students review concept maps and update information following a science conversation or activity. Depending on the amount of time we have available and students' attentiveness, I may save organizing our ideas and making connecting lines until later in the day. When we update our concept maps, we use the students' ideas (the sticky notes), a black marker, and loops of masking tape for the connecting words (e.g. like, because, have). Often I would build a "practice concept map" after school and then deconstruct it. The following day, I assist the kindergarten students with connections. This also depends on the time of the year and the dynamics of the classroom needs; some students or classrooms need more assistance with recognizing connections. First grade students would often build their concept map following the science conversation or later that day. This may also depend on the amount of time available. I never want to stop a good conversation.

FREQUENTLY ASKED QUESTION: WHEN DO I USE SCIENCE
CONVERSATIONS IN A UNIT?

Science conversations can be held at any time throughout a science unit. In my class-room, science conversations are held prior to all activities and immediately following many activities. These activities may be experiments, book looks, observations, guest speakers, field trips, projects, or storybooks. We also conclude all units with a science conversation, reiterating big ideas and highlighting important concepts. Kindergarten and first grade students participate and assist with building our concept map that visually organize our conversations.

A "look" into how a kindergarten unit "Push and Pull" evolved using science conversations:

Day 1:

The first day of our science unit begins with a **science conversation** on any ideas students want to share on "push and pull" (the students completed the oral pre-tests the week before). Most ideas were examples of objects that a person can push or pull. I wrote all students' ideas on post-it notes and later sorted the sticky notes into three groups on our blank **concept map**: examples of push, examples of pull, and conflicting ideas ("?"). Considering the conflicting ideas and unit goals, I designed the first lesson to investigate weight in relation to pushing and pulling.

Day 2:

Experiment: This lesson began with the students sitting at their desks. Using a large laundry basket, one student volunteered to push and pull the basket as I added books/weight to the basket. Following that investigation, I began adding students to the basket, and provided them with different turns to both push/pull the basket and also sit *inside* the basket. During this experiment, I brought up ideas and asked questions: "I notice Susie is slipping around, why is that? Why is Susie having a harder time pushing than Bobby? Is it easier to push or pull? Look how Susie's body is positioned and then watch Bobby." The kids excitedly joined in our **science**

discussion during the experiment. One student switched out of his snow boots to wear his shoes "better grippers". To finish this lesson, I stepped into the basket and sat down; four students were necessary to push and pull me across the classroom floor. We discussed my weight, positioning of the students' body and hands, and one student also commented on "needing wheels to push me". We ended our experiment with a **science conversation** (students sat in a circle on the carpet), and I wrote down their ideas on post-it notes. I organized the concept map later in the day (this specific group of students needed assistance with organization and connections) *without* linking words or the headings (I wanted to involve the students with adding and building the concept map). Throughout this experiment, students engaged in conversation and demonstrated enthusiasm. Later that day, I took their pictures while sitting inside the basket, printed them off, and had the pictures pasted on the cover of their journals.

For an extension activity, we read the book *Stuck in the Mud* by J. Croser and S. Vassiliou (1987). We had a short **science conversation** following the book about the plot, connections to our science experiments, and additional thoughts regarding push and pull. I mixed up the sentence, "I am stuck. Get me out!" and required individual students to cut, sequence, and confirm the corrected order prior to gluing their work on a large piece of construction paper. Above their correctly ordered sentence, students depicted a scene from the book; Ellie the elephant getting pulled out of the mud by a tractor or a monster truck.

Day 3:

The next day, we **reviewed** the experiment. This evaluation was helpful for all students, particularly the students absent the previous day. Using the same laundry basket, we also tested the student's idea of pushing and pulling myself using wheels. We placed a scooter under the laundry basket with me sitting inside it … this was VERY scary, but the kids loved it and we were able to test their ideas. We participated in a **science conversation** to review, re-iterate, and share thoughts and conclusions. We immediately updated our concept map; I presented the BIG idea at the top of the paper," Movement of objects are caused by a force", and explained science vocabulary words; the students helped connect the linking words and headings to their ideas using loops of masking tape and a marker (Figure a below). We wrote our **claim** together, "I claim that surface matters"; based on the students' thinking, activity level, and time restraints, I allowed the students to copy my words, but required an individually drawn picture to coincide with the claim. Students had to verbally share with me the picture they were going to draw before completing the work at their tables.

Later that day, we further explored the effects of the surface when pushing and pulling. The students independently worked at their tables sequencing "fast to slowest" pictures. During this independent work activity, I called one group of students at a time to come back to the carpet and skate using paper plates (I preferred wax paper but did not have any in the classroom). Students put their foot on one paper plate and pushed their body with the other foot. Students tried two different surfaces; the carpet and the tile floor. We shared our experiences with a **science conversation** following the activity.

Day 4:

We began our science block today with a story, *The Enormous Carrot* by Vladimir Vagin (1998). We discussed how the characters used their body weight and examined the story's relation to our previous experiments Students wrote claims regarding "body weight when pushing and pulling" in their Push and Pull journals. One student wrote," I claim that it is easier to use your body weight to push and pull". The picture drawn with their claim reflected the evidence; four kids pushing me in the basket, or a picture from the story we read. Later, we read the book The Giant Carrot by Jan Peck and Barry Root (1998) and created a Venn diagram (Figure 3b - below).

Day 5:

The next day we began our science block by reviewing the concept map. The concept map demonstrated remaining questions on how "speed" connected to our big idea (I had reviewed the concept map the previous evening and gathered materials for a potential lesson). More experimentation with "speed" and its connection to the big idea would develop a deeper understanding and create a more comprehensive concept map. After reminders on turn-taking and group procedures, students returned to their tables and used the materials provided (chalkboards and mini-cars) to test the different cars using the board for a ramp. After the experiments, the students shared their ideas during a **science conversation**.

Later that day, students had the opportunity to test their claims using the same materials. Each group of students were asked to predict "which ramp would make the car go the farthest; high ramp, medium ramp, or low ramp". Using post-it notes on a simple graph I charted their predictions. One student predicted medium, one predicted low, and the rest of the students predicted the highest ramp would make the car go the farthest. We tested our claims as a group. I held the chalkboard at different angles and the students sat at their tables. I asked various volunteers to help mark the distances and release the mini-truck. We discovered that the truck was possibly too heavy or awkward for the test. It kept nose diving and crashing, so we decided to use a race car instead. The results improved, but did not coincide with our initial claim, confusing the students. A little girl spoke up and said, "maybe you are holding the medium one too high and the high one way too high." This was a moment to make any teacher glow. I told her to grab three different sized blocks to prop the ramp up so "we can be more consistent with our testing". We tested the ramps again, and this time the highest ramp went farther. After several more tests to confirm our conclusions, we moved to the carpet to discuss our final claims. We discussed the claim, and I wrote the words on the chart paper. Then, I handed the students their journals. Students wrote one sentence for their claim and drew a picture for their evidence. I have learned that my emergent writers avoid frustration when requiring one sentence and a matching picture.

Day 6:

We started our science block today with a **science conversation**. This "recap" is an excellent way to focus students and review key concepts. Following today's science conversation, students completed a science worksheet, rating pictures of different sized ramps, to determine which would cross the finish line first, second, or last. On the back of these worksheets, students drew pictures of a fast ramp and a slow ramp (only two students did not draw the picture correctly). Later we read Chapter two out of the book *Push and Pull* by Vijaya Khisty Bodach (2006) and did the suggested experiment. Students wrote in their journals about "lighter objects not needing a lot of force". Many students used the word "claim" without any prompting (very exciting teacher moment). The "evidence" was a drawing of our experiment.

Day 7:

Today, we read Chapter three in the book *Push and Pull* by Vijaya Khisty Bodach (2006), and investigated push and pull trying the suggested experiment in the book using rubber bands. After this whole group investigation, we tested our thoughts with the game of tug-of-war. I used a jump rope in the classroom and explained safety lessons on strength and pulling (I performed a brief demonstration with another student). I prompted the four students on each side of the jump rope to "take one step back.... another, another, now pull!" The first person over the tape on the floor lost the match; we had a lot of fun with this activity! We conducted a quick **science conversation** at their tables to re-iterate ideas (we used the ball as a reminder on listening and turn-taking). The students wrote in their journals and drew pictures of tug-of-war; many students included "big muscles on their arms" and wrote the claim, "I claim that *strength* is needed to pull harder". Today's activity with tug-of-war was very successful, and we decided to attempt another match of tug-of-war using a thicker jump rope.

Day 8:

Today was the second tug-of-war match. This tug-of-war match was less successful; the kids tugged so hard that they hurt their hands. We went back to the classroom and ended our unit with a final **science conversation** and reviewed our concept map for any "missing elements".

In Figure 7-3, there is an example of a finished concept map from a Kindergarten unit on Push and Pull Unit. The big idea is stated at the top of the concept map with black lines and "linking words" (e.g. like, affected by) connecting student ideas. The different colored post-it notes represent the different days we updated the concept map. Also in Figure 7-3 the students created a Venn diagram of two books related to the push-pull topic. After reading these two books, the students discussed similarities and differences. The students drew pictures on post-it notes and organized this Venn diagram.

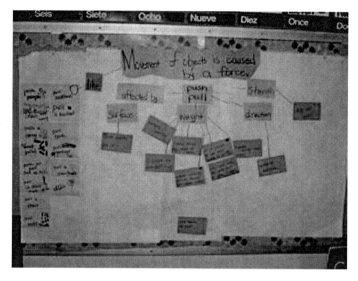

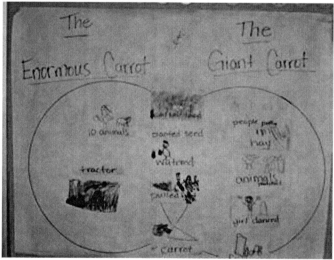

Figure 7-3. Finished concept map for a kindergarten push and pull unit.

THE EXTENDED BENEFITS OF SCIENCE CONVERSATIONS

As the school year progresses, we expand "science conversations" and accompanying SWH methods into other areas of the curriculum. After storybooks, math activities, language art activities, social studies/field trips, students are eager to share ideas using our "science circle" practices. Students demonstrate stronger skills in the areas of inquiry, self-directed learning, writing varying pieces other than "me stories", connecting and organizing ideas, and learning with peers. When asked questions, students are ready to find the answer. One day a student was hanging from our bulletin board and the clip broke. I rhetorically commented, "How am I supposed to fix this clip." Instantly I was showered with student ideas and solutions... "Mrs. Sander! Mrs. Sander! I have an idea. Do you have super glue? Do you have a new clip? Let's see if it still works!" The classroom responded and the students were eager to tackle this learning experience. These are my most rewarding and inspiring moments. Every year, I witness children of five and six years of age take up the problem solving skills they have learned from the SWH curriculum and apply them to their everyday lives. I know I have given them valuable skills for today... and more importantly foundational tools for a lifetime of learning.

REFERENCES

Bodach, V. (2006). *Push and pull*. Logan, IA: Perfection Learning.
Croser, J., & Vassiliou S. (1987). *Stuck in the mud. Magic Bean series*. Flinders Park, South Australia: Era Publications.
Gallas, K. (1995). *Talking their way into science: Hearing children's questions and theories, responding with curriculum*. New York, NY: Teachers College Press.
Esbensen, B. (1993). *Sponges are skeletons*. New York: Harper Collins.
Norton-Meier, L., Hand, B., Hockenberry, L., & Wise, K. (2008). *Questions, claims, and evidence: The important place of argument in children's science writing*. Arlington, VA: NSTA Press.
Peck, J., & Root, B. (1998). *The giant carrot*. New York: Penguin Putnam, Inc.
Sander, J., & Nelson, S. (February 2009). Science conversations for young learners. *Science & Children Magazine*, 43–45.
Vladimir, V. (1998). *The enormous carrot*. New York: Scholastic Press.

Julie Sander
Independent Consultant
Boston, MA, USA

PEGGY HANSEN

8. CLAIMS AND EVIDENCE FROM THE 5TH GRADE CLASSROOM

I have always had a passion for science, but found it difficult to get students excited about it. Textbooks weren't exciting, and the teacher directed experiments were great for me, but not exciting for the students. I use to come up with at home projects for students to do. They would bring them to school, and we would have little competitions. The students were excited about these, but that was only once in awhile. This was the way science needed to be taught all the time. Then came SWH and the classroom became the science lab that students couldn't wait to work in each day.

The last three years my 5th grade classroom has changed drastically compared to the first 20 years of teaching. The first 20 years of teaching my classroom would have had desks in rows facing front, so that talking was not encouraged. The students sat and listened, and I talked. Success would have been high pencil paper test scores. When my principal would walk in, she would have seen students working indepen-dently and silently. A silent classroom was an effective classroom. Student talk would have been cheating. Commercial posters on the wall would have shown them what they were to know in the unit. That was the teacher-centered room, where I controlled everything. At least that was what I thought.

Through my instruction in the SWH approach my classroom has become more student centered. The desks are arranged in small groups to encourage table talk. The noise level can get excited and is a consistent hum. The walls are covered with student's work reflecting how they're learning is changing throughout the unit. The big idea is posted big and bright and the student's questions are listed on the wall. I still display posters, but only as we consult experts for further information on their claims. The kids are the center of attention. My role has been the manager of the classroom to the learning coach. Now success to me is hearing what they know, not the student guessing what is in my head. They're excited about their ideas being valued, not about being right or wrong. They know they are going to learn. The thrill is the journey, not the pencil paper test.

The science textbook we used drove what was being taught. We studied things chapter by chapter. This was the only book that was used, and maybe we would watch a movie along with the chapter. We would read the book, do a few worksheets and take a test. The number of concepts taught in a year was determined on how many chapters we finished. The average length of time to complete a chapter was two weeks, and then the students would regurgitate the information on a test.

B. Hand and L. Norton-Meier, (eds.), Voices from the Classroom: Elementary Teachers'
Experience with Argument–Based Inquiry, 87–95.
© 2011 Sense Publishers. All rights reserved.

Now I use the concepts found in the Iowa Core Curriculum to drive my instruction. Instead of teaching fifteen topics each year I now teach four concepts. I teach for deep student understanding. For example, my district purchased a curriculum that included three teacher manuals for science. For my life science manual there are six chapters on six topics. Theoretically I was responsible for teaching eighteen topics in 180 school days. That is ten days per topic. I knew in my heart that kids couldn't learn "Chapter 1: Cells to body systems" in ten days! Through our study of the Iowa Core my only big idea for life science is now "The body has systems that interact together." Because this is only one of four big ideas I cover in science, we are able to spend nearly 45 days learning this at a greater depth. This has not only changed my classroom, but all elementary teachers in our districts. It has forced us to talk about the big ideas and what we want the kids to know and understand.

The materials we use in the classroom are another change since I began using the SWH approach. The textbook is only used as reference material. We have twenty to thirty books about the concept around the room at different reading levels. I borrow these from the Area Education Agency and the school media center. Some are from my personal collection that continues to grow. The kids are thrilled to bring in books from home on the concept. These books are available to read and look at for months at a time and anytime during the day. Even though our time to study a concept may end the kids know they can keep reading and learning as long as they choose.

As I end my 23rd year of teaching, science now is taught the way it should have been. It is about science being active-physically and mentally. The students get to discover how things work and why. They talk about what they think. They can't just spit answers out. They have to be able to justify and back up what they say. It is difficult for the students because they have been given answers for so many years. We in education complain kids can't think, but really, we haven't asked them to. The Science Writing Heuristic approach has helped me to provide opportunities for kids to think critically on a daily basis and love it!

SWH CONNECTION

Several years ago my school's professional development was on the 6 Traits of Writing. I was given information about SWH being offered at the Area. Education Agency that summer. The connection of 6 Traits and SWH went together so well, that I thought this would be an exciting class. I had doubts about being able to teach through the SWH method. It seemed so overwhelming with all that had to be done to teach science this way. Then one day in professional development we watched a video of another teacher using SWH. She was doing something I had done in my classroom before, but it was student-centered activity instead of teacher led. As I watched this video, I kept thinking to myself, "I can do this." I loved seeing the students doing the activities and having to figure how to do it on their own. The teacher was the coach. She was asking what they thought and why they thought it. They were not given step-by-step directions or answers. By the end, they came up with the same results as if they were given the directions, but they figured it out on their own. They had a sense of accomplishment.

Getting students excited in science is so easy with the SWH approach. The problem is not what I will teach them to get interested in this unit, but how much time do I have to teach what they want to know. Too many times what we teach in school is what is in the book. Deciding what will go into my lessons now is determined in part by the students. So each year part of it will be different depending on the questions asked by that year's class. We still learn what is required in the curriculum, but questions developed by the students will be different with a different group of kids. Questions that students come up with come from personal interest. One unit of study in 5th grade is how our body systems work together. Students have questions about everything from Down syndrome, aneurisms, and cancers, to why do you sneeze? These are of considerable interest to children that hear things at home or have had a family member experiencing them. Getting to learn something they want to know increases their interest in being at school. These are things that help me plan what I need to do next in planning what topics to cover in a unit.

CLAIMS AND EVIDENCE

Claims and Evidence is an extremely valuable piece to SWH. Both are related to the question the student or class have chosen to investigate. Students are explaining their "scientific guess" to the question or trying to answer the question. In my classroom, an initial claim shows previous knowledge on the concept we are studying. This is not the final answer, but will be what they reflect back on to see how their ideas have changed. This is an excellent opportunity for the teacher to see just how well the students understand what they will be working on. I have students write this claim in pen. I had found they don't like to be wrong, so at the end of the investigation when they were to write how their ideas have changed, they always had the right answer the first time. They just erased the first answer and changed it to what they found out in the end. They want to say they were right. With it written in pen, they can see how their ideas have truly changed.

Evidence is the story that tells about the data. I find this the hardest part of the SWH approach to get the students to understand. They want to say, "see data" as their evidence, but data alone is not evidence. Data is based on observation and can come in many different forms. What experiment you are doing will determine what form the data needs to be collected. Sometimes it might be written observations of what they see or how something works. Other forms might be a chart to record specific numbers or the times the experiment is repeated. They might also include a graph to compare the work they have done to see results easier.

After the data is collected, we need to reflect on what it means. How does it help us to support our claim and answer our question? So we work on how to tell a story with this information. When students understand the data and can tell the story this becomes their evidence. Questions they can ask themselves include: What is this data showing me? How can this tell me something? They might also say how their previous knowledge helped them determine their answer. It is essential to get the students to see a difference in data and evidence. They can spit out data without understanding. The evidence shows the critical thinking needed to apply and synthesize.

To start the year I work with students on how to make a Claim and make the distinction of data verses evidence before starting a unit. One of the things I do is use a book called *Dr Xargle's Book of Earthlets* by Jeanne Willis and Tony Ross. This is the story of an alien professor teaching his class about the strange lives of "Earthlets" (human babies). Dr. Xargle describes all the things an Earthlet does. As I read the story aloud, without showing the pictures, the students try to figure out what an Earthlet is by using information they hear in the story. When I finish they gather their clues and discuss it with their group. They will then make a claim about what an Earthlet is, and provide evidence that will prove their Claim. We share these claims and evidence to negotiate what is an Earthlet. The kids are always amazed although they heard the same story, each group analyses the data in different ways. Therefore, they come up with different evidence. This is a helpful activity to break down the process in making a Claim and to back it up with Evidence.

Another activity I use is a mystery bag. Students will bring in something from their summer vacation in a paper bag, or I will put items in bags. We pass each bag around, and they can examine each bag. Their question becomes what is in the bag. They record their observations about the bag to make a Claim. This activity gets them to use all their senses in making claims, not just sight. We will share what clues we have about each bag, and then make a claim (educated guess) about what is in the bag. Listening and debating with other groups leads the kids to wanting to gather more data. They beg to be able to use scientific tools such as rulers and balances. Groups have asked to borrow magnets. Some groups have even requested to use hammers to smash the bags or to put the bags in the freezer. I say to yes to any test that is safe and doable.

The mystery bag activity and Dr. Xargle are ways to figure out how to provide evidence instead of just giving data. Students are confident in guessing what is in the bags, so by asking questions about how they know what is in the bag gets them thinking about evidence. I also encourage them to think about their own experiences. What do they already know that might help them to connect to the data to make their evidence even stronger?

In Dr. Xargle, evidence that an Earthlet is a baby includes, a baby wears diapers, and drool is on everything and drinks from a bottle. To make this the evidence piece, they need to tell it as a story. For example, I have a younger brother, and when he was a baby, he drooled on the floor and me all the time. He had to wear a diaper and drank from a bottle, so the Earthlet is a baby. This helps students see the difference between a list of data points and when data helps tell a story, therefore, data becoming evidence.

LEARNING FROM ONE ANOTHER

How we work on claims and evidence has changed over time for the better. Students write their initial claim individually. This is a claim based on any previous knowledge they have or their best guess. We talk about how scientists often don't know a lot about the concept they are studying. So it is more beneficial to have questions than right answers. This is comforting to most students, but has often been a struggle for the high achievers who want to know the answers to memorize for the next day.

When I first started using this approach I had students work mainly with a single partner. As they worked through different experiments, they talked with just one other person. There wasn't a lot of questioning or ideas that came with this method. Sometimes the failure rate was higher, because it was easier to give up then be able to come up with a different way to look at things. The quality of claims was not good, and they had a hard time providing evidence that backed up their claims. We would write their claims and evidence on paper to present to the class. Then each pair would get up in front of the class while the rest of the class sat at their desk. The class could not see what was on the papers and so we spent a considerable amount of time repeating ourselves. Students at their seats would be off task and playing with things at their seats. Many times the evidence did not back up the claim. We did not discover answers on our own and most answers were discovered after consulting the experts.

Then I decided to have students do more in groups of 3–4. This increased the ideas in what to do and more questions about why they were doing it. Table talk was better than one on one talk, because they did question each other more. With only one other person, it was easy for one to dominate the conversation or one would just give in to the stronger voice. Word choice improved with the group because they would question what was being said if they didn't understand or agree. As a group, they would work on their claims after completing their experiment. In the group there had to be some negotiations to come up with one way to explain the answer to the question. Groups would write their claim and evidence on construction paper. This was a little better than regular paper, because it was bigger and a little easier to see by the class. The problem with this is they wanted to spend more time on decorating and writing in many colors for fun. There wasn't as much effort put in on the quality of the claim and the evidence to back it up. After spending a class period coming up with claims and preparing presentations, they weren't done with their claims but had lots of art work on the paper. We continued to present in front of the class with the rest of the class at their seats.

Now the size of the group will depend on the activity. The biggest difference is we spend more time with table talk. The desks in the room are in groups of four or five. So if there are two groups at the table, those two groups will talk about things, before it comes to the large group. Some other questions can be asked and worked out in a small group. The quality of claims is improving with the time students can question and talk.

Evidence is getting better too. I continually have to remind the students that the evidence is not data. They need to use the data to "tell a story", incorporating the data to support the claim. The use of the book, *Dr. Xargle's Book of Earthlets*, has been very helpful in learning evidence also. Students are able to retell parts of the story, so this makes sense to them easier than just using the word evidence.

The greatest benefit to me by changing the group sizes is that I feel it has increased student learning. Being able to negotiate with a variety of people allows kids to consider many alternative explanations. Listening on their negations provides me with information about what they know and don't know. I can use this information to provide additional learning opportunities.

NEGOTIATION CIRCLE

The best adjustment I have made to improve class sharing of claims and evidence is sharing in a class circle. During our SWH development, we experienced debating claims and evidence in a circle rather than one group presenting at a time. The conversation was natural and passionate. The flow of ideas definitely bounced from one learner to another, rather than from teacher to learner. Everyone seemed to be engaged in the conversation. It was fun! I knew I wanted to try this with my kids.

At my first opportunity, I asked students to push back their desks and to circle up their chairs. My directions to them were to listen and question to understand. They did not need to raise their hands, but practice good listening skills so they could jump into the conversation at the appropriate time. I challenged them to be able to talk to one another without me having to contribute heavily. I wanted them to see me as a learner also. We would be debating our ideas as a way to understand, not for the point of arguing. They could use their journals to help them justify their claims and note questions they want to ask other people.

Our first negations circle went well. More conversation took place. More students participated. Kids questioned one another. They had fun learning from one another. In a recent negotiation circle, we were answering the question of, "where does digestion begin?" Three groups came up with digestion begins in the mouth, while two other groups said it starts in the stomach. One group was backing up their claim by explaining that when the cracker was in their mouth for the minute it began to get mushy and watery. They believed it was beginning to digest, because we talked about digestion was the breaking down of food. Another group questioned this, because they knew there were juices in the stomach that helped break down food, so that was where they thought digestion began. One student said, "Digestion begins in the mouth, but continues in the stomach. That is why it is called the digestive system! That means it takes place in more than one place. A system is a group of organs that work together." She said it so confidently and with passion it was an "AHA!" moment for our class.

This example is why I love having a negotiation circle rather than groups presenting their claims and evidence. I think it leads to greater conversation, not just sharing like show and tell. We carry on a conversation with a group of people, like that at the supper table. Students don't need to raise their hands, and they need to listen to each other to know when they can interject. My main role is to make sure the discussion stays to remarks on if the evidence backs up the claim and if the claim answers the question. I write previous claims on the white board so the students can see them and refer to them without having to have the group repeat over and over.

The thing I like the most with the circle is everyone stays on task longer. When they aren't sitting at their desk, there are fewer distractions. They are more willing to talk, because they are all facing each other. No one hides so they don't have to talk. It amazes me how a student that is typically quiet in other class discussions, opens up when in a circle. We also get other questions that we can explore that go along with the opening question.

In another negotiation circle we explored the question, "How does participating in different activities change our heart rate?" We did five different activities, (laying, sitting, standing, walking and running) in class and found our heart rates for each one. Students came up with their claims in their groups and we shared in our circle.

While working in their groups, other questions came up that they included in their evidence. Because they have the opportunity to talk and negotiate, they are able to come up with more findings than just the one question. These questions will be addressed when consulting experts to find out if their findings are correct.

One group stated that the boys in their group had higher heart rates than the girls. So they believe that there is a difference in heart rates between the sexes. Their evidence was that during the exercises performed the three girls' average heart rate was slower than the two boys' heart rates. Even though the question was about how different activities changed heart rates, this group came up with deeper information that will be explored using experts.

Another group made their claim that the more physical the activity the more their heart works. They stated that they thought the heart and lungs worked together. Their evidence was that when they had to breathe harder, take deeper breathes and their chest moved more, to run their heart rates were higher. At this point in our unit, we have not made the connection of the circulatory system and respiratory system working together. They made a generalization about this and the other groups weren't so sure about it. The group provided evidence by telling how their data showed that there is a connection between the lungs and heart.

Another group came up with another finding when recording their heart rates at different times of the day. Their initial claim was the harder the activity the faster your heart beats. They also stated that if you get excited or anxious about things, your heart rate would go up. The evidence they provided was from data they collected on their own. One student took her pulse while we were taking Basic Skills Test. She found that her heart rate was higher at that time then when we were not taking the test. Another student shared that he remembered that his heart beat faster when he was nervous about performing in front of an audience.

When we finish in our circle, we review the claims and find similar things that were said with each group. We had very similar claims to the question we started with, that when we increase the level of activity the heart rate went up. We still needed to consult with experts because we needed to see if the three new ideas were true.

Not every conversation leads to consensus claim and evidence—we don't always agree. The purpose of the conversation is for students to wrestle with what they think they know. If those ideas aren't consistent with current scientific understanding, dissatisfaction grows in the student, so they want to know more. It usually leads us to more information and questions to be answered.

After having conversations around the claims and evidence, we consult the experts. Consulting the experts is a way for students to compare their thinking with what scientist think. It is an excellent way to incorporate literacy with science. In addition to the 20–30 books around the room, there are computers for students to use. They will search to find if their claims are true and to see if these new ideas are true or not. Also, we will Skype experts outside our area. Speakers and video clips through services such as United Steaming act as experts. I try to have students consult a variety of experts. In this way they are able to strengthen their reading, writing, listening, speaking and viewing skills.

After consulting the experts students negotiate with one another and can revise their claims and evidence. They also reflect on what they learned by looking at their initial claim. They will add to their journals on how their ideas have changed. I feel it is necessary for students to know their learning changes over time.

Claims and evidence can be used in more than science class. I have incorporated this language into other subjects during the day. I thought if getting students to talk to each other and solving problems worked in science so well why not try it in other subjects? I tried it in math and it worked extremely well. When starting new concepts I will write several examples on the board. In their groups, they will talk about what they see and make a claim. The best example came from studying multiplying with decimals. For years they wanted to drop the decimal straight down like in addition. For the first four lessons this would work, so they had a hard time understanding that the decimal moved because of the numbers behind it. When I had problems that the decimal couldn't drop straight down it took a lot of discussion to find this out. The results when they came up with the rule of multiplying decimals compared to me just showing and telling them were huge. Their daily math scores and their long-term memory of how to use them lasted throughout the year, not just until the test was over.

I also use the SWH method to teach social studies. Finding out students' previous knowledge allows us to move farther than we would have if I just started where the book says to start. Kids know so much from watching the Discovery Channel and using computers we need to find out what they know and move on. Claims and evidence has also played a prominent part in my social studies. Because my students are experienced in considering alternative explanations, they read accounts of historic events with a different perspective. They often will questions authors because of apparent biases. They know that different books can have different answers. They tend to want authors to back up their claims the same way they do in science. Even though an event might have a specific set of data points there might be multitude of interpretations. This is an excellent example of the difference between data and evidence. Students see that although people experienced the exact same event in history they all walk away with individual stories. We moved from seeing the value of dates and people to understanding themes and consequences. We also understand the significance of consulting the experts. We often can consult primary sources in recent history and those primary sources are many times people we love.

The most recent learning of mine that has been beneficial in the classroom is the use of literature in conjunction with science. This has been exciting. I will teach an English lesson to show ways writers write to help readers, and the science lesson can be to consult the experts. After listing all the different ways the authors made the information look important, students can find answers quicker and easier because they know what to look for. They can also show this by writing like the author to express what they think is important. This is an area I want to learn more about and incorporate into the classroom as I continue to be an SWH teacher. I know that we use literacy to learn any subject matter. Tapping into opportunities to teach and access literacy across all content, will be more beneficial for my kids.

The Science Writing Heuristic approach has not only impacted me, but more importantly my students. The confidence and knowledge they have gained through this approach is incredible. They ask questions of themselves and others. They answer question confidently and are able to back up what they say. They know their ideas are important. They value the ideas of other people. They are able to see connections instead of isolated facts. Most importantly they are thinkers and learners. Now I share my passion for science with my kids.

REFERENCE

Willis, J. & Ross, T. (2002). *Dr Xargle's Book of Earthlets.* London: Andersen Press.

Peggy Hansen
Griswold Community Schools
Griswold, IA

CARRIE JOHNSON

9. HIDE AND SEEK AND THE AIR IN THE CLOSET

Environments for Learning

On a recent road trip, my family and I were playing oral word games to pass the time. During one of these games, where someone states a word and the next person has to think of a new word that starts with the last letter of the previous word, my turn came up and I considered words that began with 'e.' The draft for this chapter was taking shape, and the word 'environment' came to mind. I stopped the game just briefly, and turned to my 9-year old daughter who is in an SWH classroom. To my question, "how would you define environment?" she responded: "Where something lives. There can be different kinds of environments, like jungles or deserts, and animals and plants live in certain ones because of special parts they have that help them live there." Adding his thoughts to the discussion, my 11-year old son stated that an environment is "a place where you have everything you need to grow and survive." Probing further, I asked my daughter to describe *her* classroom environment and she shared the following: "Well, a classroom is where humans work together to learn things. We use special tools in our classroom, like notebooks and pencils when we observe things. These special tools help us learn things. We collect questions and then we put them on the computer. We do research in books and the internet to answer our questions. We talk to each other a lot about what we are thinking and the information we find. Our most important tool is our brains." My daughter's responses spurred thoughts of classroom visits I have made over the past three years as an educational consultant supporting SWH teachers. Let's visit a few of these classrooms.

A PEEK INTO SWH CLASSROOMS: CLASSROOM 1

After a brief review of yesterday's activity with a guest speaker, kindergarten teacher Mrs. Northrup directed the students' attention to the class concept map titled "Weather Affects Us". This generated negotiation among students about the learning, and how it should best be represented on the concept map. 'Buzzing' began, and after partner talk, discussion opened to the entire class. I worked to keep up as student statements "I agree because" or "I disagree because" took the conversation back and forth from student to student and occasionally student to teacher. Teacher questioning led the students to consider converging 'evidence' from student comments. Eventually Mrs. Northrup made a summarizing statement from all the responses. She asked the class to consider if the statement represented the thoughts and ideas from

B. Hand and L. Norton-Meier, (eds.), Voices from the Classroom: Elementary Teachers'
Experience with Argument–Based Inquiry, 97–106.

the group conversation. Additionally, she asked if there also were any ideas needing further exploration. General consensus was reached, and Mrs. Northrup invited the students to return to their tables and record individual reflections of their beginning understandings of the big idea. The promise of an investigation later in the day to extend and/or revise their current understandings closed the lesson. An excited learner immediately shouted: "I am *SO* glad I'm not sick today!"

A PEEK INTO SWH CLASSROOMS: CLASSROOM 2

In a recent visit to a first-grade classroom, I arrived just a little late for the observation, and planted myself in the back of the room and set up my laptop. A review of yesterday's science lesson was taking place. The teacher and students were reading from the class concept map stating the big idea "living things have needs for survival." The words food, water, air (oxygen), shelter (protection) and sun were webbed around the big idea. Off to the side, the question "Does a plant need sun to grow?" was posted. Underneath were two ideas students had generated for testing this question. "1. Put a plant in the sun, by the window. 2. Put a plant in the cupboard." As the two statements were read aloud, the teacher asked the students to consider how they would go about answering the question through each of the experiments. A lively discussion ensued, as students debated which experiment would work the best and why. As the conversation progressed, I listened in amazement while these first-grade students, with minimal teacher involvement, shared ideas about the concept of experimental design. Throughout the discussion, the teacher prompted, restated, and questioned to clarify thinking. At the conclusion of the conversation, students had reached a consensus. The class agreed they could feel confident in their design if the only difference in the experiments had to do with the amount of sun each plant received. I was already reeling from the AMAZING discussion amongst these young learners, but there was more to come.

One child suddenly brought forth the concern that there might not be air in the cupboard. He shared that this would make both sun and air factors in the experiment. Others pondered his concern, generating a 5–6 minute conversation from the class about air, including ideas that air is all around us and that we can't see air. At the conclusion of the conversation students were unsure about what this concern might mean for their experiment. The teacher, listening in up to this point, decided to send the students back to their seats to see how writing might shape their thinking. She asked them to decide at this point where they might place their individual plants, in the window by the sun or in the closet without. In addition, she asked them to make a claim about what they thought would happen to the plant in their chosen location.

While students were writing, this gave the two of us an opportunity to discuss how we might proceed. We discussed Skyping a high school science teacher, consulting a book, carrying out an experiment with a candle in the cupboard. In the end, the teacher decided to have the students finish preparing their plants, write and share their writing with a partner, then come to the conversation circle for large group sharing of claims. This accomplished, the teacher began the conversation by reviewing ideas about air that had been previously discussed. Then the three children who decided to put theirs in the cupboard spoke about their claims. As the first boy spoke about his claim that the plant would grow because of the shelter, air, and water, another boy spoke up excitedly. "I have the answer about air," he shouted. "I play hide-and-seek a lot and when I hide in the closet I can still breathe, so there HAS to be air in the closet!" The teacher asked the rest of the class to consider this, and if they could agree as a group that this is true. The class accepted the child's statement and decided that with either experiment the plant would get air. The teacher ended the lesson for the day by thanking the students for their respectful negotiation, and the young hide-and-seeker for taking a risk by sharing his thinking. New insights, as well as lingering questions from the day's events were added to the concept map for continued pursuit.

A PEEK INTO SWH CLASSROOMS: CLASSROOM 3

In a school on another visit, I was sure I had the time right, but as I popped my head in the kindergarten classroom a second time to begin my SWH observation, I had trouble locating the teacher. I observed small groups of students working at tables and some groups on the floor. There was a focused busyness to the groups' activities, and the multiple conversations elevated the noise level to a productive hum. It turns out the teacher had been there all along; I finally found her, sitting on the floor with a group of students who were negotiating where to sort objects on their living/nonliving chart. The teacher was listening in on the discussion, and hearing polite disagreement leading to placement of most things in an agreed category, she moved on to another group.

A PEEK INTO SWH CLASSROOMS: CLASSROOM 4

On yet another school visit, the evidence of science learning lined the hallways. Bulletin boards displayed throughout captured my attention, demanding pause and observation. At each board, I took in the stated learning objectives from which science units were developed, the student writing of their understandings of these objectives, the photographs taken of students conducting experiments or researching and writing, and the written reflections of teachers and students throughout the unit. Outside of the classroom I was visiting that day was a small table with nonfiction books and artifacts from the current science unit. A message posted above read, "We are learning how we use our senses to explore our world." The halls and walls of the entire wing of that building proclaimed the message to its visitors that the pursuit of science ideas is valued, fun, and worthy of sharing with others.

Beliefs about teaching and learning play out in the day-to-day life inside a teacher's classroom, and evidence of these beliefs permeates his or her classroom environment. In the SWH classrooms where teachers embrace and approach decision making through a learner-centered lens, we see, hear and feel differences in the classroom environment from classrooms where traditional science teaching and traditional inquiry occurs. A teacher's view of who controls the learning in the classroom influences the way that teacher organizes the environment for learning. In the SWH classrooms I've had the privilege of visiting over the years, here are some key characteristics that describe those learning environments.

STUDENT-CENTERED LEARNING

To embrace the SWH as a way of teaching is to embrace the idea that the learner, not the teacher, is in control of learning. An activity often used with beginning SWH teachers invites them to consider skills we have developed and those we have not, and the conditions that have been present or absent for us in learning new skills. The result of the activity is always a revelation - that most key characteristics for learning cannot be controlled by the teacher. (For information on this activity see Appendix A in *Questions, Claims and Evidence* (Norton-Meier, Hand, Hockenberry, Wise, 2008). I use the word revelation, because the engagement with this activity creates a pause for teachers to consider the degree to which their classrooms are aligned with ways in which people learn. Reflection around teaching and learning becomes transformational, as described by the teachers' stories in this book. When teacher decision-making is aligned with how students learn, planning and implementation of all classroom activities results in changes to classroom climate, organization of materials and physical arrangement of the room, and interactions.

The SWH is often described as science inquiry with embedded literacy concepts, and embracing how students learn is the foundation the approach is built upon. The very nature of inquiry is advanced when teachers acknowledge that students are in the driver's seat where their learning is concerned. Student-centered learning promotes motivation and engagement, and allows students to pursue learning that fits their learning style. A common response from beginning SWH teachers when confronted with the concept of inquiry and student-centered learning is to question the role of the teacher. Teachers often confuse inquiry and the phrase 'student in control of their learning' with the concept of 'anything goes.' This is far from what occurs in the SWH classrooms. A teacher **does** have a role in learning. A teacher establishes a safe, accepting climate. A teacher structures interactions that promote student-to-student talk. A teacher used questioning skills to advance discussion. A teacher organizes time to promote exploration of science ideas through investigations, discussion, and research. A teacher listens actively and enters the learning opportunities strategically to foster increased conversation, present an alternative idea or question or summarize learning. If you are reading carefully, you will notice I have not yet used the words 'teach' or 'tell.' These roles are less likely or not likely at all to promote the SWH approach, because emphases on both place the focus on the teacher as knowledge-keeper. As you have been reading in teacher stories, this approach is about *students* as knowledge-*developers*. It is likely clear also as you have been reading, that teaching through the lens of student learning is personally fulfilling to both students and teachers!

The teacher authors of this book lend their voice to the great rewards of the SWH implementation. In the remainder of this chapter, I will lend my voice to the rewards of teaching and learning through the SWH approach as an outsider looking in their classrooms. My experience as a consultant visiting both SWH and non SWH classrooms affords me the opportunity of making key distinctions among the learning environment in traditional science and the SWH classrooms. The culture and climate, sights and sounds of the learning environment, the ways teachers organize and manage time and space, and the interactions in the SWH classrooms are described in the remainder of this chapter.

CULTURE AND CLIMATE

Relationships matter, and the establishment of positive ones for learning is the environmental backdrop in the SWH classrooms. Relationships play out in the persistent development of a climate and culture of mutual respect and trust, high expectations coupled with nurturing support, honored individualism, safety in risk-taking and exploration, and the recognition of the value and worth of each student's thinking and learning process. Failure is seen as a positive. Teachers view themselves as learners along with the students, adding to the safety in risk-taking and developing ideas, in learning from trial and error, in exploration of inquiry. Because the classroom climate exemplifies the above characteristics, interpersonal skills are developed naturally, through speaking, listening, rephrasing, questioning, taking turns, and disagreeing respectfully.

ORGANIZATION AND MANAGEMENT

As was evident in the second story in which I described finding the teacher moving around the room to groups of students working at tables or desks clustered together and around the room on the floor, the SWH classrooms are organized to provide spaces and structures for collaborative group work. Throughout the SWH approach, students learn from each other. As opposed to single rows of desks all facing the front of the room where a teacher typically stands and delivers instruction, in the SWH classrooms one is likely to observe settings that promote conversation, such as a circle of chairs or a large open space for students to sit in circles on the floor, and clusters of desks together. Additionally, spaces for individual and small group activities such as observation, writing, and research, are created. During science time in the SWH classrooms, a visitor would notice less of everyone engaged in the same activity at the same time, such as reading from the same textbook, writing from a prompt, or copying information from an overhead or whiteboard. A more typical observation would be to observe individual and small group work occurring simultaneously, with students involved in activities such as journal writing, observation and data collection, student read aloud, and experiments.

In my work with SWH teachers, I can comment on one additional consideration of organization and management related to a teacher's daily schedule. I have learned from working with both beginning and veteran SWH teachers that their approach to planning differs from traditional science teachers. As an SWH teacher initially plans and begins to implement a unit, science concepts guide teachers toward a big idea. (You may want to refer to the chapter on concept maps for specific information on how a teacher uses his/her own concept map to develop the concepts embedded in the science unit). This changes the focus on teaching many facts about a variety of topics to deeper conceptual learning. To accomplish this, science time is afforded longer blocks of time. As described earlier, the structured collaborative inter-actions merit adequate and connected chunks of time to develop an understanding of concepts. This connection of content to concept not only increases time available for learning science, it increasingly dictates connections across content. Veteran SWH teachers organize for learning around blocks of time for whole group, small group and individual learning opportunities. This planning approach differs from traditional teacher schedules chopped up by set amount of times for individual subjects in isola-tion. Additionally, with the SWH approach, development of a science unit shifts from all the planning of activities and lessons done prior to starting the unit, to adjustments made daily during unit implementation. These adjustments of concept development and activities and lessons are based on beginning and growing understandings of the students as they engage in the unit.

PHYSICAL ENVIRONMENT

From the many stories and descriptions in this chapter and others, I hope you are gaining a picture in your mind of the sights, sounds, and feelings of the SWH class-rooms. In this photo of one SWH classroom, the students' learning journey is evident (See Figure 9-1). Question charts, created by the entire class and individuals and small groups are displayed around the room. Claims and Evidence posters are posted to show the thinking of students from their inquiry and investigations. Concept maps showing the students' growing understanding of the big ideas are prominently dis-played. The concept map is a **multi-modal** representation of the thinking, reflection, and understandings of the class. Nonfiction book collections clearly identify the science ideas being investigated. There is a range of topics, authors, and reading levels represented in the books. They are placed around the room and easily accessible to students to promote research, writing, discussion, and pleasure reading. The SWH classrooms contain more than print. You may see a 'research' corner where laptops are available for viewing videos or DVDs, creating PowerPoint, word-processing, or Skyping with other classrooms and science experts. Science notebooks are on top of desks, showing students' growing understanding of the big ideas.

A key difference of the SWH vs. traditional teachers I easily observed when I first began supporting the process, was the student ownership of the room. Student thinking is all around the room, and when I walk into an SWH classroom, I easily identify what science ideas they are studying. I think back to my very first classroom, where mass-produced teacher-store artifacts adorned my room. Looking back, students rarely referred to all those artifacts, and I used only some of them for instruction. They took up space on the walls and reduced the student ownership of the learning environment. What a shame I did not realize at the time I did not need most of those artifacts - I just needed the students. What I could have done with the amount of weekend time preparing my first classroom, not to mention the money I spent at the teacher store!

Figure 9-1. One example of evidence related to learning in an SWH classroom.

INTERACTIONS

Interactions among teachers and students in classrooms have the potential to either increase and enhance learning experiences, or decrease and diminish those experiences. In many traditional classrooms I observe, patterns of interactions do little to bring voice to the individual ideas and enthusiasm of each learner. A typical interaction goes like this: the teacher poses a question. Multiple students raise their hand. One student is called upon, and the teacher either affirms the answer or gives the 'correct' one. Observing this pattern repeated over one large group/class setting and throughout the day, one would be hard-pressed to dispute the claim that this type of interaction stifles the thinking of most students. As concerning, is the danger of students developing the habit of mind that there is one correct answer. Worse yet, that there is one way of thinking about an idea, and that answer is to be ultimately found with the teacher. A potential consequence of this pattern in traditional teaching is for a handful of students to be called on, leaving the remaining students' thinking and voices to be silenced. Here ended the inquiry!

"The SWH approach is intended to promote both scientific thinking and reasoning in the inquiry experience, as well as **meta-cognition**, where learners become more aware of the basis of their knowledge and are able to monitor their learning more explicitly." (Norton, Meier, Hand, Hockenberry, Wise, 2008). Towards this end, the types of interactions I commonly observe in the SWH classrooms differ greatly from the above described. For example, I cannot always easily track with my eyes which child is speaking, because I do not always see students raising their hands. Rather, I hear conversation move from student to student, back and forth, sometimes will little or no teacher interaction. As in the second classroom example where the teacher was not easily observed in the midst of the highly engaged student learners, another descriptive characteristic of teachers of the SWH classrooms is the ratio of their talk to student talk. It can be said that teachers 'get out of the way of learning' by talking less and listening more; questioning more and telling less. "Teacher as listener and observer" is a common phrase I hear used to describe the role of the teacher in an SWH classroom. I have collected data on talk patterns in order to provide feedback to teachers, and as implementation of the approach increases, the ratio of teacher talk to student talk represents more student talk. Not only does this teacher behavior benefit student learning by promoting multiple perspectives to be heard to enhance individual reflection and understanding of science concepts, it affords the teacher a rich formative assessment opportunity, not just in terms of science content, but additionally related to speaking and listening skills.

The "agree-disagree" interaction is another commonly observed interaction in the SWH classrooms, and quite easy to establish. The strategy used to set up this interaction is that a student, group of students, or the teacher presents an idea to their audience - partner, small group, or class. The audience then responds with "I agree because" or "I disagree because." This structure affords benefits to both speaker and listener. The speaker thinks about their understandings of the science ideas and how best to communicate them. To do so, key skills such as summarization, analysis, and synthesis of ideas are necessary. The listener takes in the information, compares and contrasts it against their understanding, and makes an affirmation or revision of thinking. Regardless of the outcome (affirmation or change to thinking), this interaction facilitates key communication learning outcomes identified through most state curriculum documents. The process of negotiation- interacting with knowledge from self and others to arrive at a deeper understanding – is used throughout the entire approach, and the "agree-disagree" can be easily used to structure opportunities for negotiation.

Negotiation is central to the SWH approach. "Students need the chance to analyze their evidence, discuss an initial claim, analyze the evidence again, talk, revise their claim, talk, revise their evidence, talk, write it all down, analyze it all again, erase, talk, write, talk, and the process continues." (Norton, Meier, Hand, Hockenberry, Wise, 2008). The think/talk/write/talk interaction is evidenced in the SWH classrooms by the use of individual student science journals, group reflection charts and concept maps, question charts, lab materials and observation corners, and the physical arrangement of the room with clusters of desks and large spaces for conversation circles (See Figure 9-2).

You may be reading this and thinking to yourself, "Yeah, but I've seen these things in teachers' classrooms I know who are not SWH teachers" or "I do not use the SWH approach but you would see and experience many of these things in my classroom." If this is true for you, the reader, congratulations! You align your teaching practices with a learner-centered belief system, the very foundation for the SWH approach.

Figure 9-2. Students engage in a conversation circle.

It is true, the SWH approach, in the words of a first-year implementing teacher, "is just good teaching and learning!" If you as the reader find yourself further away from the classroom environment described in this chapter, take heart. Read to learn how teachers are working to establish environments conducive to successful and empowering learning experiences for each and every student in their classrooms.

CHAPTER SUMMARY

The descriptions of the SWH classrooms from this chapter evolve initially during science time given the SWH approach is an approach to teaching science. As student response to the approach leads to increased student ownership and accountability for learning, a learner-centered belief system drives teacher decision more holistically. Changes from traditional teaching become evident across the entire school day. In summary, some expected changes in the classroom environment from a traditional science teacher to an aspiring SWH teacher may include:

- Student-centered learning – the teacher acts primarily as a resource in helping students find answers to questions and solutions to problems, as opposed to giving directions and providing answers.
- Relationships and culture for learning – each student experiences a sense of belonging and the entire class is a learning community where inclusiveness is a core value and an established practice.

- Organization and management – the driving force behind time management and grouping is the student-driven outcomes from their inquiry and the necessary collaborative opportunities to pursue those outcomes across the school day, incorporating the natural use of language, math, and science to learn about the world. Students work individually, in small groups, and as an entire classroom learning community.
- Physical arrangement – clusters of desks promote the think/talk/write interactions. The walls describe the 'how' and the 'what' of the students' learning journey. A wide variety of nonfiction books and other media resources are prominently displayed around the room and provide access to ongoing research.
- Interactions – All interactions, student-to-student and teacher-to-student, are structured with intentionality and care. Think/talk/write is a common interactive pattern. High expectations for learning are the backdrop for each structured interaction.

What students need to learn is likely to constantly change as the world around us changes. *How* students learn will remain the constant. Eric Hoffer (July 25, 1902 – May 21, 1983), an American social writer and philosopher said, "In times of change, the learner will inherit the earth while the learned are beautifully equipped for a world that no longer exists." This profound statement celebrates the essence of the SWH approach and its influence on classroom environments.

REFERENCE

Norton-Meier, L., Hand, B., Hockenberry, L., & Wise, K. (2008). *Questions, claims, and evidence: The important place of argument in children's science writing.* Portsmouth, NH: Heinemann.

Carrie Johnson
Green Hills Area Education Agency
Glenwood, Iowa, USA

CHERYL RYAN AND GINA JOHNSON

10. LITERATURE AND WRITING ARE BIG "ADDITIONS" TO SCIENCE

2 Classrooms + 2 Journeys = 4 Fold Learning

A WALK THROUGH

Anyone stepping into our classrooms before or after school can see exactly "what" our students are learning by observing several student work areas. They would see items such as a concept map, sticky notes, article clippings, posters, diagrams, and more on our science bulletin boards to show where their learning is leading them. Most of the features on these bulletin boards are student made. The concept map is the key feature that provides us with clues about where the learning will most likely go next. We can then provide supplies and materials to help them continue their learning journey and discover their next piece of evidence to support the "big idea" on their concept map (See Figure 10-1). Sticky notes become the holding tank for key questions that help connect these newly learned pieces. Students love to personalize these pieces through independent projects and group work by creating posters and diagrams that highlight their experimental findings and research.

Beyond the bulletin boards, many other parts of our classrooms serve as breeding grounds for learning. Our counter tops are often cluttered with experiments, and rarely are any two alike! Materials and supplies for these experiments can be found in our classroom cupboards, but occasionally, students will bring things from home to use in their experiments. These student-designed investigations either help support or alter their thinking, but they are always purposeful and try to answer a particular sticky note question. Guests in our classrooms will also find tubs full of books related to the current unit of study. These can be used as research tools or as evidence to further support their findings. Students keep records of their learning in a journal. These journals contain combinations of drawings, diagrams, paragraphs, and data, which show changes in student learning. In a sense, it is their personalized knowledge map. These journals help us determine what a student knows and how far that learning has progressed over time. Although these are an excellent gauge of learning, they are not the only source we rely on. Laptop computers serve as efficient tools for collecting evidence, but they can also be used to create graphs, diagrams, reports, web quests, power point presentations, and opportunities to communicate with scientists and students from other schools.

What might not be as evident to a guest is "how" students are learning. In order to understand this aspect of the SWH approach, a person would need to be present during the school day. Several times each week, students engage in conversations about their

B. Hand and L. Norton-Meier, (eds.), Voices from the Classroom: Elementary Teachers'
Experience with Argument–Based Inquiry, 107–123.

Figure 10-1. Physical science unit concept map.

learning. Sometimes these conversations are argumentative because separate student investigations did not all lead to the same conclusions. Just as adult scientists look at data critically and reason through their findings, students must go through this same process. As teachers, it can be difficult at times not to interject into student negotiations. Although this may seem trivial, it is incredibly important not to interfere with this powerful learning process. Students have a remarkable ability to sift through contradicting pieces of information and form logical explanations for their differences. The more students engage in this process successfully, the higher their critical thinking and reasoning skills become. Ultimately, this all leads to relevant, permanent learning. What a person will not see much of in our classrooms are textbook and worksheet based lessons. Textbooks are used merely as resources; they do not drive instruction, nor do they deem the importance of what students need to know. Though this seemed unsettling when we first started, we quickly saw the value of high level inquiry learning.

HOW WE GOT STARTED

In the spring of 2008, we were asked if we would be interested in participating in the SWH grant along with five other second and third grade teachers from our school. Compared to many schools in Iowa, ours is large with nine to ten sections of each grade level and 25–29 students in each classroom. We were excited to be included in such a small group of colleagues, and we were particularly intrigued about where this would lead us.

We began our learning by completing a one-week summer course, which required us to submerge ourselves in the SWH process primarily as learners. At the end of the course, we found ourselves to be teetering on an edge between frustration and excitement. We left having far more questions than answers! Upon returning to the classroom, these questions led to a big case of anxiety about being able to carry out the SWH approach.

As we started our first unit, we were constantly questioning what to do next and how to approach it. We were full of uncertainty about how to develop student concept maps, how to word questions to stimulate students' thinking, how to get students to create questions, how to facilitate discussions, and how to support students with investigations. What we failed to realize was that this was new to students, too. Once we acknowledged this, we began to settle down and focus instead on what we were seeing and hearing that was working in our classrooms.

Communication between us was critical, but there also came the realization that our classes were each going in different directions with their learning (in other words, their interests were leading them to separate areas of the concept map). This created uneasiness because it was hard to plan collaboratively. We slowly learned to relax and let the students pull us through the unit. We used several of the same activities, but at different times to coordinate with the natural progression of student learning. For example, one of our classrooms most pressing searches was to find out what the Sun looked like on different planets, while the other classroom was trying to figure out why the moon does not always look the same. Using a large, round sculpture in the center of our school commons area, an activity was set up around it to help students visualize the Solar System. The round sculpture became the Sun, and a roll of toilet paper that had been marked "ten million miles per square sheet" was unrolled from it. The students marked where the planets were located, beginning with Mercury on the fourth square all the way out to Pluto on the 400th square. The students then used cardboard tubes as telescopes to examine the magnitude of the Sun. Their journey began on Mercury, where the "Sun" was much too large to be seen in its entirety and ended at the end of the roll on Pluto, where it barely took up a tenth of their telescopic view. Because of the success of this activity, it was saved in case the other class might find it useful. Sure enough, a few weeks later the second class utilized the materials to find out why Mercury's orbital time was so much faster than Pluto's. They lined up on the marked toilet paper as though they were the planets and began rotating and revolving around the Sun while staying in their orbital paths. They quickly discovered how much faster it was for the inner planets to make a revolution than the outer ones!

As the unit continued to unfold, we found ourselves using one another's activities at different times to answer various questions, not set ones. In doing so, we discovered how much these activities could enrich our learning environments while decreasing the amount of teacher preparation time. Our collaboration changed dramatically during the unit; it went from trying to make daily lesson plans together to brainstorming activities and how many ways they could be diversified to help students learn and connect ideas. Although this transformation was uncomfortable for us as teachers, we realized we were making notable strides in creating student-centered classrooms.

WHY DOES SWH MATTER?

From an engagement standpoint, it matters. If you ask any student what they like about science, they will almost surely say "experiments." Before we were introduced to this approach we were doing experiments in a traditional manner. We were supplying materials, designing the experiments, and instructing students on how to complete them to answer a specific question. Rarely did an experiment end with varied results. We were assured of the outcome and needed little time for students to reflect on the results. Using the SWH approach, students no longer have to endure teacher driven experimentation. They have been freed to explore questions that are relevant to their personal understanding and make connections to the big idea. Whole class experimentation has been redefined: students contemplate and develop questions they want to find answers to, form small groups, design their own experiments, make claims, and collect data to support their claims. Students then negotiate these findings as a class, so everyone has opportunities to share and learn from one another. For example, when a class had lots of questions about the ability of solids to turn into gases, they were given inexpensive air fresheners (the kind with the pull-up top that exposes gel to the air). These air fresheners were cut into approximately two inch long by one-inch tall sections. Students were then asked to write questions to help them decide what conditions would turn solids into gases. All of the questions were recorded on a whiteboard and grouped into categories. Each category then became a carefully molded question. Here are some of them:
– Does it make a difference if the pieces are in a closed or an open container?
– Which will evaporate faster, a whole piece or a cut-up piece?
– Will salt speed up evaporation?
– Will being under water slow evaporation down?
– How does wind affect evaporation?

Each student then chose which question they wanted to seek the answer to and formed small groups of two to three students (there were ten groups altogether). They designed experiments around their question, developed recording charts for their data, and carried out their experiments over a two-week period. When the experiments were stopped, the class got together to talk about their findings. What resulted from a two-day conversation was amazing! Groups investigating the same question might have done very similar experiments, but had different outcomes (this would have never happened with a teacher designed, whole class experiment). Their conversations centered on controls, variables, and how matter changes. As a teacher, it was wonderful listening to all of the thinking and learning going on. Students didn't even want to go to lunch until they were satisfied that they had the answers they needed!

WHAT DOES ASSESSMENT LOOK LIKE NOW?

Assessment using the SWH approach is also different. Their increased knowledge is evident in conversations and negotiations, but capturing it to share with parents or to use when assigning grades for report cards is a little trickier. We have written pre and post tests, but these do not always reflect the multitude of information students have obtained. We often give these tests verbally in an interview format to remove the reading and writing barriers, especially for special education students. Formative assessments, such as unit journals are like windows in time; they document shifts in thinking and new learning over the course of the unit. Projects, experiments, and discussions are also used to assess students' progressions in thinking. Another piece of assessment on the "big idea" comes from a final reflection, which is presented in an alternative way (such as a poster, song, or video) rather than a standard paper and pencil test. For example, students wrote a readers' theater to share what they had learned about the big idea: "Matter can exist in different states." Before students could start writing, they needed to look at various readers' theaters to see what they all had in common. Students came up with the list in Figure 10-2.

Another essential prewriting step was having students write statements of learning about the big idea. Students had opportunities to reflect on what they learned individually, in small groups, and as a class. These statements of learning were typed and projected onto the whiteboard, so students could discuss and negotiate throughout the process. This work was printed out for each of the small groups to use during their writing process. Four other adults were recruited to help (a special education teacher, an associate, an instructional strategist, and an associate principal), so each group had someone to facilitate the process. Each adult typed the ideas that students generated. All of the groups were supplied with sticky notes, graphic organizers (labeled: ideas, characters, setting, problems, etc.) for note taking if needed, a copy

---

Readers' Theater.....A Closer Look

- Need a topic

- Can be several pages in length

- Characters or Cast ex: Narrator

- Title

- Authors names listed

- Makes sense....exciting for audience

- Punctuation does not need to be at the end of every part (someone else can continue the thought)

- All parts can read at the same time

- Expression....change how the words are written ex: bold, italicized, all caps, or underlined

- Use different punctuation (! ? .) to show feeling

- Can include a list of the authors other readers' theaters that he/she has written

---

Figure 10-2. Ideas for creating a reader's theater script.

of our statements of learning, and our poster about readers' theaters. The students came up with their ideas quicker than anticipated and were highly engaged in the process. When students had questions, the entire group could be seen running back to their concept map or referring to nonfiction texts in the back of the room. Each adult's role was merely to type and encourage participation from all of students in the group. It was startling to see the high interest and excitement in students of all abilities. When the groups finished, they practiced each character's part before choosing their own to perform. Students practiced their readers' theater to insure proper fluency and expression. Each of the five groups performed for other third grade classrooms and for their families. Seeing the excitement, pride, and ownership the students felt was astounding and priceless as a teacher. In Figure 10-3 is an example of one of the five readers' theaters.

The Three Matter Brothers

By: Drew, Reese, James, Lawrence, & Ryan

Characters: Solid-Liquid-Gas (The Matter Brothers)-Narrator 1-Narrator 2

Narrator 1: A few years ago the Matter Brothers got into a fight at their house, which was a huge mansion. The fight began when Gas told Liquid that he could turn him into a gas. Let's see what happened.

Gas: I can turn you into a gas.

Liquid: Oh no you can't. I've been a liquid all my life, and I love it. You cannot turn me into a gas.

Gas: Oh yes I can. I just learned about your particles. If I heat you up, I can turn you into a gas and you would be just like me!!

Liquid: (getting all ready to fight) I would like to see you try!!

Solid: (walks into the room) Calm down you guys. What are you fighting about?

Liquid: Gas keeps saying he can turn me into a gas. I don't believe him!

Solid: Well, Liquid, that IS true.

Gas: I told you, I told you!!

Liquid: I don't believe you guys. I have always been a liquid.

Solid: We can prove it to you if you want.

Narrator 2: So Solid and Gas, determined to prove Liquid wrong, began to show Liquid how he could be turned into a gas. They put him in a pan and put him on the stove with a fire underneath. Liquid, although nervous, allowed them to put him over the fire. It wasn't long before Liquid noticed a change.

Liquid: What's happening to me? I feel different. My particles seem to be spreading apart. I feel light, like a feather.

Narrator 1: Liquid rose up out of the pot and became hard to see. He was now steam, which is a gas.

Figure 10-3. (Continued)

Liquid: I know, I know, I'm sorry I didn't believe you. You were right; by heating me up you changed me from a liquid to a gas. I always wondered how it would feel if my particles were all spread out. (crying) I feel nauseous.

Gas: You'll get used to it. You'll feel better soon.

Solid: I'm a little jealous. Do you guys know if you can turn me into a liquid?

Gas: Hey, do you think you could turn ME into a liquid?

Narrator 2: They spent the next few days in their messy mansion trying to figure out if a gas could be turned into a liquid and if a solid could be turned into a liquid. Do you know if a gas or a solid can be turned into a liquid???

ALL: THE END!!!

Figure 10-3. One example of a reader's theater script created by our students.

LITERATURE CONNECTIONS

We clearly see how introducing literature tied to the big idea impacts students. It serves as a tool to enrich discussions, promote inquiries, and spark ideas for experimentation. When carefully planted throughout each unit, literature helps inspire students to keep searching for answers. A bonus we have discovered is how the overlapping of subjects significantly increases learning connections through cross-curricular ties. Because of this layering, time constraints are eased, and students can effectively "lose" themselves in their work. This extra time allows them to dig deeper and make solid, permanent connections to multiple subjects. Our students aren't sure where we are at on the agenda because they can't differentiate between the science and literacy lessons! Literacy connections are a natural fit with science. For example, while working on the big idea, "Objects in the sky have patterns of movement," a Native American story was introduced. The book *Thirteen Moons on a Turtle's Back*, by Joseph Bruchac, is a story about the thirteen moons of the year. Each moon has a poem that tells a story.

The students paired up to practice reading a poem and needed to get a mental picture (visualization) of what the poem was describing. Each student was given a shell from the turtles back to illustrate what they had visualized their poem to be about. The class compared the two shells drawn by students and the illustrations from the story. This led students to see how the cycles of the moon change throughout the year. It also served as a springboard to other poetry books about the moon including, *Full Moon Rising* (by Joanne Taylor) and *When the Moon is Full* (by Penny Pollack and Mary Azarian). Students had explicit instruction and various activities over different types of poetry including, haikus, couplets, and cinquains. Students then chose a type of poetry to write and illustrate. This would serve as a reflection of their learning at the end of the unit. They also had a class poetry reading to share the poems they had written about "objects in the sky and their patterns of movement (See Figure 10-4).

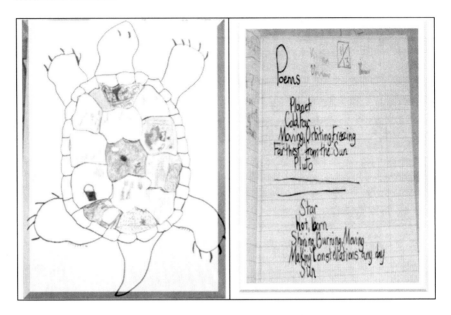

Figure 10-4. Illustrated turtle shell and student poetry.

Postcards from Pluto: A Tour of the Solar System, by Loreen Leedy, was another piece of literature that tied directly to our earth science unit. This book creatively captures its readers by displaying postcards from each of the planets and the Sun as though they were being visited by people who were on vacations. Each postcard is uniquely designed and contains many interesting facts about our solar system. These postcards easily tied to letter writing, and they had perfect timing within our building; our fifth graders were learning about the universe and we thought they could benefit from a review of the solar system. The students chose one of the planets or the Sun, researched to find several intriguing facts, and created a unique postcard of their own (See Figure 10-5). When they had finished composing them, they illustrated one feature from their writing on the backside. The postcards were then sent to fifth graders. We were pleasantly surprised to receive personalized postcards back a few weeks later. These provided us with more information about the planets, the Sun, moons, asteroids, and galaxies. As the students shared and compared their postcards, several discussions ensued that helped students piece together key concepts in their studies. This pen pal relationship not only made learning fun, but it challenged students to take on many roles during their learning (researchers, authors, illustrators, and negotiators).

Using a quality piece of literature can also be a vehicle to introduce a science concept or to help reinforce a skill. *Dear Mr. Blueberry,* by Simon James, is a book used in our classrooms to help with the big idea "Plants/Animals have unique structures, which have functions that help them survive in their environments." The vocabulary words "structures" and "functions" are difficult for students to understand.

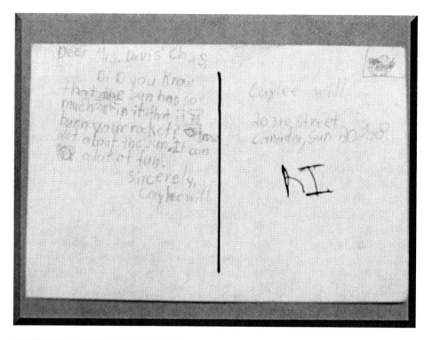

Figure 10-5. A student postcard with information about the sun and an illustration of its location.

After reading the first page, students were left with the question "can whales live in Emily's backyard pond?" Many students could quickly answer "no." However, other than "whales are too big and need salt water," the students couldn't think of other reasons why they couldn't live in that environment. After the students write in their journals about their thinking, they begin to search for their evidence. In small groups, students had three note cards labeled: structures, an arrow symbol, and functions. Students came up with various structures, which they wrote on note cards and placed under the structures column. They then wrote the functions of these structures and placed them directly across from the structures in the function column. Students were highly engaged as they moved their desks together to make their columns longer and longer. All groups took turns sharing out, so they could learn from one another, and a list was created on a chart. The next step was to distinguish between a structure and a unique structure. The ones the class felt qualified as unique structures were starred on the class chart. We sat in a circle and had a class negotiation about how their new information concerning whales affected their opinions when thinking about a whale's ability to live in Emily's backyard pond? Each student had something to say, and finally had a deep understanding of unique structures and functions (See Figure 10-6).

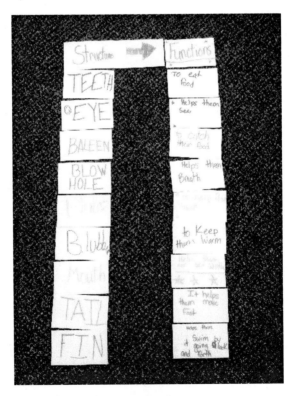

Figure 10-6. Structures and functions note card activity.

Whale blubber, being of particular interest to students, led us to take a closer look at it. Exactly what is blubber? Do we have blubber? They knew that it kept whales warm, but how? Students put vegetable shortening on one of their fingers and placed it into ice water along with a second bare finger. They instantly discovered how effective blubber is at keeping whales warm in cold ocean waters. They loved the messy investigation, and in the middle of the activity, someone yelled out "It's FAT!" We finally finished reading *Dear Mr. Blueberry* and were excited to see that some of the aspects we talked about during our research and negotiations were revealed secondly in the story.

EMBEDDING TARGETED SKILLS

Teaching reading skills with science gives students access to real life applications. Many primary classrooms use PWIM (Picture Word Inductive Model) to develop students' vocabulary, as well as sentence and paragraph structures. Our classroom used a PWIM poster, but not in the usual way. Rather than "shaking out" words, categorizing words, writing sentences, organizing them, and writing paragraphs, we used them to practice the skill of fact and opinion. Our science bulletin board had a PWIM poster on it of elephants in their environment. Students could easily "shake out" elephant structures (ears, tusks, trunks, etc.), but they didn't know the functions of these structures. Students used nonfiction text to research the structures and discover the functions that help them survive in their environment. Rather than write words on the poster, fact statements were written about an elephant's structures and functions during their research process (See Figure 10-7).

Figure 10-7. PWIM poster used for finding unique elephant structures and functions.

Some topics are more abstract than others, making it more difficult to bring alive for students with investigations. These topics are easily researched. Students need to be able to consult with what other authors have written in order to come up with evidence for their questions. Therefore, it is necessary for students to know how to find quality non-fiction texts and use their text features. Students who are able to use text features can locate information efficiently and have an increased understanding of an author's purpose.

A quick formative assessment to discover what kids know about text features can be developed using quality non-fiction books. One way we did this was by giving small groups an envelope containing a photocopied page from a nonfiction book with a different highlighted text feature on it. The groups were asked to brainstorm why authors would use their particular text feature to help readers and then share that reasoning with the class. A corresponding poster (with copied pages of various text features) was made and hung on the bulletin board, so students could write the purpose of each one on it. This activity helped students discover various text features as well as learn how to navigate and find information efficiently. The use of text features is a stepping stone not only for learning new information, but also for learning how to organize information and write like an author (See Figure 10-8).

Another way to inject literature into science is to form high interest book clubs. Students who show a deep interest in a specific area of the concept map can choose

Figure 10-8. Poster with text features.

to work together to research a subtopic and create a reflective piece to share with the class, such as a skit, a poster, a book, a song, a model, a video, a power point, a demonstration, or whatever they can come up with. For example, a group of students was interested in finding out what functions tails had for different animals. They were given a collection of non-fiction books. Each one was different, yet somehow related to the others (i.e. birds, amphibians, reptiles, mammals, and fish). Special consideration was given to individual student's reading levels. The group skimmed the books, looking at text features and illustrations. Each student then wrote a question and start reading portions from any of the relevant books to answer it.

Once they had finished their research, the group met to discuss their findings. Then they began the process of negotiating how their research fit together and how it related to the big idea this process can be slow, so be patient. As a finalization of their project, the group created their own concept map on tails and shared their knowledge with the rest of the class (See Figure 10-9).

One final example we have of literacy in science is the making of a class book modeled after a text. Using a fiction or non-fiction text for a read aloud and think aloud is a powerful way to model fluency, comprehension, and inquiry. We have found that students love listening to us wonder about why an author did something on a certain page or throughout the book, and how the author's words made us think about something else we've learned or read about.

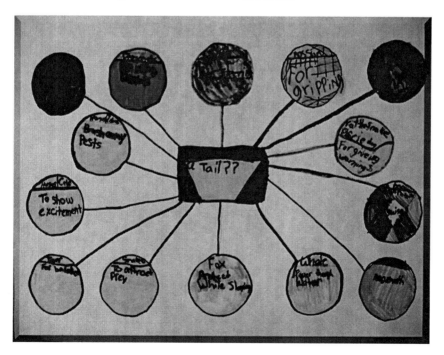

Figure 10-9. Subtopic concept map from a book club.

For instance, the book *What Is The World Made Of? All About Solids, Liquids, and Gases*, by Kathleen Weidner Zoehfeld, was read to a class. This humorous text got students thinking about how the world could be, but thankfully isn't (i.e. can you imagine a world where your shoes were made of milk?). As students listened to and laughed at the examples in the book, they began discussing why these things couldn't ever actually happen here on Earth. These discussions were directly related to our big idea, "Matter can exist in different states."

The students showed so much interest in this book that several students began sketching out their own version of it. Shortly after discovering these "gems" and asking the students to share them with the rest of the class, almost everyone wanted to make their own. In a unanimous decision, the class elected to create a formal class book. Each student chose a different object to change state and conveyed how that would affect conditions for humans in both writing and illustration (this, of course, was the fictional page). The next page became the non-fiction side of their thinking. Students used scientific reasoning to explain why such a thing couldn't happen in real life (See Figure 10-10).

Figure 10-10a. Class book based on a non-fiction read aloud.

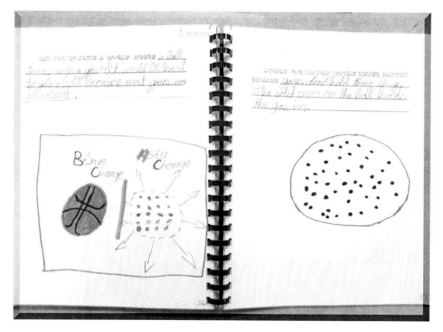

*Figure 10-10b. Student example of a basketball becoming a gas
and identification of the problem this poses.*

NEXT ON OUR HORIZON

In using the SWH approach, we have seen the importance of providing enough structure to help students make cross curricular ties, yet allowing them ample freedom to have ownership and direction of their learning. Our next challenge will be to apply this approach to all subject areas. In other words, use this science approach as though it were an inquiry "lens" to view all subjects through. We've used concept maps to document our learning in other areas (such as math and social studies, see Figure 10-11), questioning and whole-class discussions, and opportunities to find evidence through investigations.

Although we've already begun this journey, we are finding that each subject has its own unique twist that forces us as educators to take a step back and look at several key aspects. These include questions such as:

– How and what will kids "wonder" about this unit?
– What ties and overlaps can we make between subject areas?
– What key pieces of literature can we use to foster thinking?
– Can we predict what those key "a-has" will be?
– What types of investigative activities will help move learning forward?
– What will negotiations look like?

The SWH approach is a journey, which leads us in slightly different directions each year. New students, who bring new experiences to the classroom, pave separate

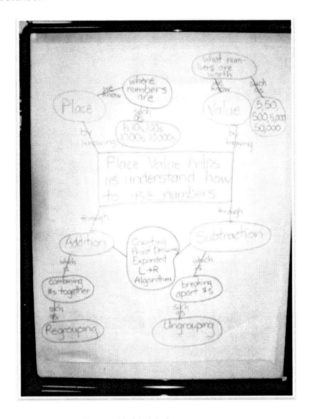

Figure 10-11. Math concept map.

learning paths from previous years. Using inquiry as our teaching focal point helps us to prepare our students to be leaders in the twenty first century. This gives them the necessary skills to become successful adults. Our overall goal isn't the memorization of vocabulary and facts to get an "A" on a test, but rather to cultivate students to ask questions, seek the answers to these questions, and take ownership of their new found knowledge. By using the SWH approach, this is possible for ALL students, regardless of their abilities. Their excitement for learning overflows in abundance without lines drawn to separate subject areas. It is an honor to be a part of something that is creating the leaders and thinkers of our future. What's humbling is that it all started with the willingness to change our way of teaching. It was truly that simple! Join us on our journey and see how adding literacy and writing to science creates authentic learning experiences for all!

REFERENCES

Bruchac, J., & London, J. (1992). *Thirteen moons on a turtle's back*. New York: Philomel Books.
James, S. (1996). *Dear Mr. Blueberry*. New York: Aladdin Paperbacks.

Leedy, L. (2006). *Postcards from pluto: A tour of the solar system.* New York: Holiday House.
Pollack, P., & Azarian, M. (2001). *When the moon is full.* Boston: Little Brown and Company.
Taylor, J. (2002). *Full moon rising.* Toronto: Tundra Books.
Zoehfeld, K. W. (1998). *What is the world made of? All about solids, liquids, and gases.* New York: Harper Trophy.

Cheryl Ryan and Gina Johnson
Lewis Central Community Schools
Council Bluffs, IA, USA

JULIE MALIN

11. WHAT'S THE BIG IDEA?

Putting Concept Maps into the Hands of Your Students

Throughout twenty years of teaching in the primary grades, my classroom structure and style of teaching has altered a little each year. I am currently teaching first grade and have an active group of twenty-two students. Knowing the days of larger class sizes are looming overhead I am grateful for my current class size. Among these students, two who are staffed with behavior IEPs (Individual Education Plans) and two are staffed with academic IEPs. I share this information so you know that this approach helps all students achieve success. All twenty-two students are present during science instruction.

MY CLASSROOM

Time was set aside three days a week in the afternoon for science instruction. The majority of our science activities and experiments happened during that scheduled time. However, that was never enough time for all of the science that takes place. As a result, science instruction gradually became more and more integrated into our morning meeting time, literacy instruction and occasionally during math. Working with the SWH approach changed this daily structure. Our science topics tended to guide, or sometimes take over, our school day. When science came up, we fit in, or wrote our ideas down to discuss later. For example, when we were learning about matter the students experimented with seeing their breath outside in the morning while waiting for school to begin. During morning calendar time we discussed temperatures and their affect on solids, liquids and gases. After this discovery we began recording the outside temperature as one of our daily calendar activities.

Nonfiction books, on our science topics, were used for whole group read alouds throughout the day and during guided reading groups. Science topics were utilized for the teacher's daily writing. Everyday at the beginning of our literacy block, I wrote a story for my students (See Figure 11-1).

Using an easel and a large sheet of chart paper, I began by modeling how to plan a story, then, I wrote. When my story was done the students and I reread it and revised as needed. Then they write a story in their draft book. Generally students selected their own topics to write about. However, there were times when I assigned topics that were science related. For those writing assignments, I modeled report writing. Student reports used a variety of formats. Students wrote standard reports in their draft book and published them. Sometimes we used pictures of animals from magazines

B. Hand and L. Norton-Meier, (eds.), Voices from the Classroom: Elementary Teachers'
Experience with Argument–Based Inquiry, 125–139.

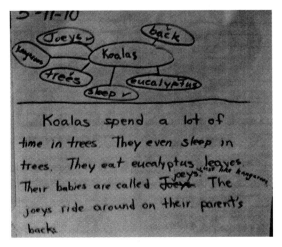

Figure 11-1. Teacher's writing demonstration.

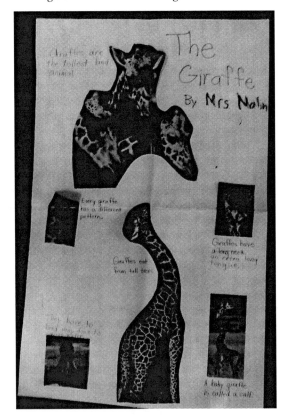

Figure 11-2. Giraffe poster report.

for their plans and then the students wrote about the animal in the picture. Posters were another way students chose to publish their animal reports. The reports became so popular many students chose to write animal reports even when they were not assigned (See Figure 11-2).

I tried integrating science into our daily handwriting practice. After students were given the opportunity to explore with magnets they were asked to recall what they had discovered discussing which items were attracted or repelled by the magnets. A handwriting worksheet listed several of the items the students had tested with their magnets. They were to practice writing the word while they identified which items were attracted to magnets (See Figure 11-3).

I created a similar activity when we studied matter. The students had questioned whether all liquids would freeze when they were exposed to cold temperatures. We made a list of liquids they wanted to test. Twelve of those liquids were poured into an ice cube tray, placed in a plastic bag and stored in the freezer overnight. Before seeing the results of their experiment, the students were given a handwriting assignment to complete. The handwriting worksheet listed all of the liquids that we had placed in the ice cube tray. The students were asked to trace and practice writing the names of the items that they predicted would freeze.

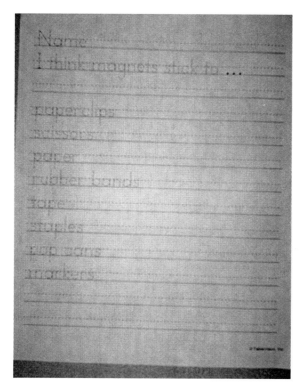

Figure 11-3. Magnet handwriting.

Figure 11-4. Questions and answers from the magnet unit.

Visitors to my classroom saw many examples of the SWH approach. Claims, questions, and evidence were recorded by students on charts or sticky notes and were hanging all around the classroom. We record what we have learned from experts and those are visible. All of these items, along with concept maps, are displayed in a corner of our classroom. When space allows, materials remain on the walls throughout the school year. Since we often find ourselves referring to a concept map or information that was recorded earlier in the school year, it was helpful to have them available. Students can make connections between different topics. For example, we began the year studying life cycles, but the students usually notice the concept of cycles repeats itself in other science units, such as the water cycle and food chains during the habitat unit. Another example of visual evidence of the SWH approach was the questions asked at the beginning of our magnet unit that were displayed on a bulletin board in the back of our classroom. As we found answers to the questions we added them to the board. Our board grew as we read books, completed experiments, and watched videos. This bulletin board proved to be a tremendous resource during our unit when we wanted to recall something we had learned (See Figure 11-4).

BEFORE THE SWH APPROACH

Prior to using the SWH approach, I used a thematic approach to science instruction. Units included insects, fall animals, arctic animals, ocean, zoo and transportation. They had remarkably little if any connection to benchmarks and standards. The units were random and had little purpose. There was very little writing, research or experimentation required of our students during science and no questioning or argumentation. We delivered the information to the students through videos and books and hoped that they would retain it.

Next, came a project type of approach. This was practiced for several years and the focus of science became reports and projects. This approach integrated literacy and science. Students had more opportunities to do research on topics that interested them. They were able to demonstrate their learning and present their projects to their classmates. Integrating literature into all areas of the curriculum has long been an interest of mine. I valued utilizing nonfiction books for a read aloud, guided reading groups, and report writing in the writing process. The Project Approach was an improvement over the thematic units, but still lacked structure and ties to benchmarks and standards.

With the onset of state benchmarks and standards in the state of Iowa our school district felt our thematic units needed to be purpose driven. We needed to create units or revise those currently used so they were more focused and met the new local and state guidelines. The SWH approach helped us begin this process.

THE SWH APPROACH

Since using the SWH approach in my classroom my instruction and planning have changed. All science topics are now driven by local and state benchmarks and standards. We identify a big idea, rather than a theme to focus our units. The big idea is used to make a concept map which guides planning and helps students make connections. Resources such as books, materials and activities, which support the big idea, are planned and resources, such as books and materials are collected or created.

Many of our units began with free exploration opportunities for students. During free exploration time, the students explored materials related to the unit. Students sorted plastic animals into different groups for our unit on animal habitats. They played with magnet toys and experimented with magnet activities for our magnet unit. After they grouped picture cards of plant, animal and insect life cycles for the life cycle unit. As they explored these items I circulated around the classroom and asked them questions about their thinking. Why did you group those animals together? Are there any other ways they can be grouped? What do they have in common? Why did you put those cards in that order? What is making those materials stick together? By doing this, I learned how much they knew about the big idea and determined our next activity. The students started asking questions themselves. We recorded those questions and attempted to answer them during the unit.

I found that first graders enjoy the SWH approach to science. It complimented their naturally inquisitive manner. They loved to ask questions and were not afraid to wonder about things. When we began our unit on animal habitats we discussed what different animals needed to survive in their own unique habitat. We expanded upon their kindergarten farm unit. We brainstormed what a cow needed to thrive in its habitat. The students asked do cows need barns? Do cows sleep standing up? Does chocolate milk come from brown cows and white milk from white cows? Since all ideas are listened to during SWH science, students feel comfortable participating.

First graders expected their teacher to have all of the answers, to be an expert on everything. They were surprised when I did not answer their questions. This was a major role shift. I had to train myself to not answer their questions. Prior to using the SWH approach I DID answer their questions. After years of teaching the same units, I had a large knowledge base. I enjoyed sharing all of that with my students and "having all of the answers". I WAS the expert. It was quick and easy to supply

Dear Families:

We are starting a project on community helpers. The students are each "interviewing" an "expert". They need to choose one person to survey about their job. The students have written this survey. We will share this information with the class so that the students can learn about a variety of jobs.

Thank You!

Community Helper Interview

Name of person being interviewed _____
Name of student doing the interview _____
What kind of work do you do? _____
Do you work for a company? _____
Do you wear special clothes? _____
Do you read at your job? _____
Do you drive a special vehicle? _____
How long do you work? _____
What time do you work? _____
What do you do at work? _____
Are you the boss? _____
Do you get breaks? _____
Is your job hard? _____
Do you like your job? _____

Figure 11-5. Community helper interview.

them with all of the answers. Now, we record their questions on a chart or post-its and then answer them throughout the unit. Recording their questions gives them value. We "check with the experts" for some questions and find the answers from books, videos, Internet or a guest expert that comes to our classroom. Other questions are answered through experiments and observations. When we studied community helpers in social studies, the students checked with a local expert. As a class, we made a list of questions. Each student interviewed a family member or friend about their job and then reported back to the class what they learned (See Figure 11-5). The students enjoyed this activity and saw experts could be someone they knew. When we shared the interviews with the class, everyone reported what their "expert" said.

WORKING THROUGH A UNIT

Our final science unit of the school year was animal habitats. Our big idea was Animals Need Things for Survival. The first activity was a free exploration activity. The students were given tubs of plastic animals. The tubs contained farm animals, insects, reptiles, ocean animals or zoo animals. The students were instructed to spread their animals out on their table and work as a group to sort them. They decided how to group them. As they sorted I circulated around the room and asked questions about their sorting; Why are these animals in a group together? How did you sort your animals? Can this animal be grouped with any other group? Once they have sorted their animals I ask them to sort again another way. Later, they moved to another table and sorted a different type of animal. They grouped their animals according to type, color, size, body coverings, how they moved, what they ate and where they lived. This activity helped me to determine what their level of understanding was and I got an idea of what type of animals interested them most. This helped me narrow down the types of habitats we would study since there was not enough time to cover all habitats. The big idea was, "What Do Animals Need for Survival," so the focus was not on all of the different habitats.

Our next activity was to make a classroom concept map (See Figure 11-6). I used the teacher concept map as a guide when developing our classroom map. To maintain student interest I selected specific habitats based on the classroom generated concept maps. I avoided spending time discussing a habitat the students already knew a lot about or had studied before.

This unit provides me with the perfect opportunity to integrate nonfiction literature. One activity the students enjoy is a habitat hunt. After reading *Walking Through the Jungle* by Debbie Harter we made a chart and list the habitats from the story and some others. The students were then given a large variety of nonfiction books and magazines about, and asked to search for animals in their chosen habitats. Students recorded the name of their animal on the sticky note and place it in their habitat (See Figure 11-7). Additional habitats were added if needed. All answers were accepted.

We left this chart up throughout the unit. Throughout instruction we were continually checking and confirming the student's initial prediction. As specific habitats

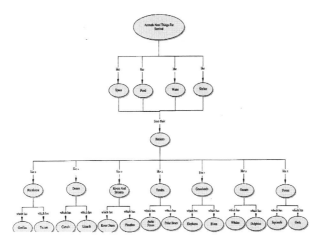

Figure 11-6. Teacher concept map.

were confirmed we removed the sticky note and recorded that animal's name on the habitat chart. This chart changed a great deal during our unit.

Another good source for habitat information was *Arthur's Animal Adventure* By Marc Brown. This book contained several basic habitats and shows animals that live in each of these habitats. We created a habitat chart using this book. Prior to reading this book we scanned for habitats. I recorded the habitats on a large sheet of paper, attached animal stickers to index cards, and passed them out to my students. When an animal was mentioned in the book, the student with the corresponding card came up to me and we recorded it on the chart in its correct habitat (See Figure 11-8).

Figure 11-7. Habitat chart developed from nonfiction book activity.

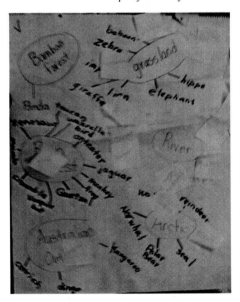

Figure 11-8. Arthur habitat book activity.

One of the highlights of first grade was an end of the year fieldtrip to the local zoo. This was the perfect activity to end our animal habitat unit. Unfortunately, due to budget cuts, our trip to the zoo was cancelled. As a result of the cancelled trip, a new ending activity for this unit was developed. I wanted the students to be able to identify the importance of different habitats for different animals and how people create special habitats in a zoo. Students used construction paper to create a habitat for an animal of their choice. Each habitat needed to include everything that animal needed to survive. I informed them that animals can share a habitat if they share that habitat in the wild. Next, we used the habitats that they created to make a class zoo. Students also brainstormed a list of what zoos need for animals and for their human visitors (See Figure 11-9).

All of the habitats were arranged on a bulletin board. Many of the projects were three-dimensional. Then we added the other items that zoos need. We also took photographs of all the students in our class in order to add people to the zoo. We placed the photographs on the sidewalks and bridges in our zoo.

To integrate social studies the students made a map of our zoo when the bulletin board was completed. We used maps from other zoos as reference. One of the maps we used was a large-scale map of the local zoo. The animals on this map are attached with Velcro. We read about each animal at the local zoo and then tried to determine where its habitat might be (See Figure 11-10).

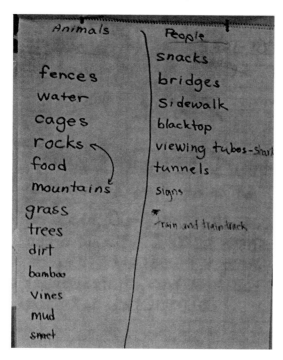

Figure 11-9. List of zoo needs.

Figure 11-10. Map of the local zoo.

GETTING STARTED: CONCEPT MAPPING

I was fortunate to participate in two different SWH workshops. During my first year of instruction there were a few other "newbies" with me. We were all extremely intimidated by concept maps. The first concept map us "newbies" made came pretty easily. We finished it quickly making one large bubble and connecting it to other bubbles. When the instructor came around he said, "that is not a concept map. That is a web!" He pointed out that we had no connecting words between our ideas. SWH was all about making connections between our ideas. We had none. We later learned that connecting words make it possible to "read" through a concept map and connect all of our ideas.

When planning a SWH science unit, the first step is to use your district's benchmarks and standards to identify the big idea. For example, our benchmark for the standard of life science was to recognize living things are found almost everywhere in the world and distinct environments support the life of different types of plants and animals. The big idea we chose from that benchmark was, "Animal's habitats help them to survive." Next, the first grade teachers and I created a concept map to identify the steps needed to successfully instruct the unit. Our concept map about animal habits began with the big idea that animals need things for survival. We listed what animals needed in their habitat, followed by some examples of animal habitats. Every individual concept was connected by a connecting word. The concept map read; Animals need things for survival like food from their habitats like a rainforest.

Although a concept map was time consuming to create, it became a wonderful planning tool to use when developing a SWH science unit. We tried to include a lot of ideas on our concept maps so we would be prepared for any direction our student's questions may have taken us. The more details that you can include on your concept map, the more prepared you are as a teacher.

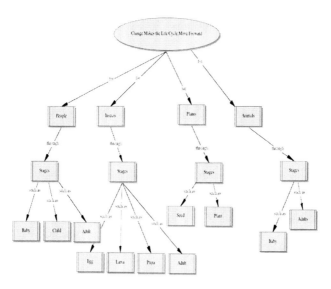

Figure 11-11. Life cycle concept map.

When we first created our teacher concept map for life cycles, we included animal, plant, insect and human life cycles. Our big idea was; change makes the life cycle move forward, so it did not matter which life cycle we studied. One class was very interested in the plant life cycle and another in the life cycle of insects. As long as both classes kept the big idea as their focus we knew the benchmark would be covered. By preparing ourselves for several possible choices the unit became more student driven and we were ready for wherever their interests led us. After completing our teacher concept map we begin collecting resources and activities to use for our unit (See Figure 11-11).

CLASS CONCEPT MAPS

A classroom concept map is another important tool for a SWH science unit. A classroom concept map is one that you make with your students. At the first grade level, most of the classroom concept maps were created as a group with the students verbally adding their own ideas and the teacher recording them. A classroom concept map can be created at the beginning, middle, or end of the unit.

A classroom concept map created at the beginning of a unit can be used as a learning tool. It can be added onto as your class progresses through their learning. In contrast, if you wait and make your classroom concept map after you have done some activities, the students may be better prepared and have more ideas to bring to the map. Finally, a classroom concept map that is made at the end of a unit shows the teacher that their students have learned and what connections they have made between concepts. When I first started using the SWH approach for my science instruction I began each unit by creating a classroom concept map with my students. I found that it was a good measure of their prior knowledge. If their knowledge of a topic was limited so was the concept map. It was very difficult to do a concept map of "The Three States of Matter" at the beginning of a first grade science unit. They had little prior knowledge.

Initially, my classroom concept maps were done at the beginning of a unit. Now I've revised my instruction and I do them towards the end of the unit as a cumulating activity. I'm interested in hearing what they have learned and how they have connected concepts together. During our unit on Matter the students always come up with creative ways to show how a liquid can change to a gas and a solid on our concept map.

No matter when you decide to do a concept map with your students it is helpful to have a list of connecting words. Generating the list of connecting words is an activity we do as a class at the beginning of the school year. This activity would take place prior to any of our science units. The teacher could make a poster with the connecting words listed or it could be a "student produced" list with the teacher acting as the scribe to give them ownership. Below is a list of connecting words a group of teachers developed at a SWH summer workshop (See Figure 11-12).

Connecting Words for Concept Maps

Contains
Includes
Made by
Can be
Such as
Lives in
Occurs in
May indicate
Measured by
Have
Like
Which has
Are
From
Is involved in
Is based on
Limits
Determines
Takes place when
Uses
Produces
Increased by
Influences
To form
Can be converted to

Figure 11-12. Connecting words for concept mapping.

My first concept map of the school year was usually teacher driven. The teacher did the recording of ideas. The students shared what they knew about the topic by answering questions. At this point many of my students had little or no experience with the SWH approach to science or concept maps. I asked the students questions concerning what they know about life cycles and what they discovered during our first few activities. If our big idea were not discovered during our beginning exploration activities, I would tell the class the big idea and write it on the top or the center of the concept map. The student's responses were recorded onto the concept map on a piece of chart paper. A whiteboard or blackboard could also be used. However, a piece of chart paper was easily moved to another location without destroying the classes' work. At this point, all ideas the students shared were recorded. If a concept map got crowded and could not be easily read by the students, I rewrote it. As we proceeded through the unit, understandings would change and we would learn new concepts. The concept map could be added to or changed. Sticky notes were helpful when creating a classroom concept map. Student's ideas could be moved around, removed or changed easily. Different colored sticky notes or markers were also useful if we wanted to add ideas to our map at a later time. New learning could be designated with a different color.

After the unit was over, if space allowed, our concept maps remained posted. During the school year my students enjoyed going back and looking at concept maps that we created earlier in the year. Occasionally, we referred to a previous concept map and connected it to a new topic we were learning. Students also enjoyed sharing our concept maps with their parents. When parents visited our classroom the maps helped them understand how the SWH approach worked. They were also excellent artifacts to use when planning for the same unit the following school year.

As the school year progresses and the students have had some experience helping to create concept maps as a group, I tried to get them more involved in making the concept map. I made a semi-blank concept map with lines and bubbles for students to record their ideas. Each student was given a copy of the semi-blank concept map. We filled it in together as a group. The more experience the students had making concept maps the better they got at selecting connecting words. By giving the students more responsibility in making the concept map they became more involved in the process and were more on task during the activity. My students with IEPs required a little more assistance with their concept maps, but by placing them near me, I was able to give them the help that they needed (See Figure 11-13).

Recently, my principal was interested in observing an SWH science activity as part of my teacher evaluation process. We were toward the end of our unit on magnets and I had been planning on doing a class concept map. However, since we were nearing the end of the school year, I was curious to see if my students could complete a concept map on their own with just a little guidance from me. Each student was given a concept map with only the big idea written on it; magnets have force. The plan was to have the class complete the rest of the concept map together. To help guide them, I recorded their ideas onto chart paper and they copied everything on their papers. Next, the students added the two types of force that we had observed during our experiments and read about during our research; repel and attract. They chose

Figure 11-13. Semi-blank concept map.

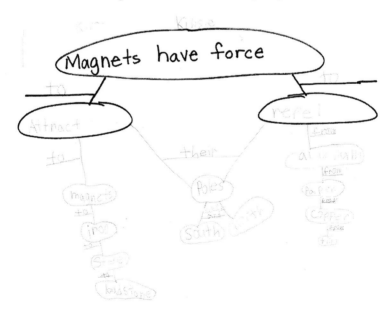

Figure 11-14. A student-generated concept map about magnets.

which connecting words they felt worked the best when we tried to "read" the map. Students continued to call out ideas for the concept map, which I would then record for them. Since they were copying the words as I recorded them the students were not focusing on the spelling of the words, but on generating ideas for the concept map (See Figure 11-14). My principal was surprised by how on task ALL of the students were during the creation of the concept map. Even students, who would normally get frustrated with a task like this, wanted to share ideas and recorded everything on their concept map. My principal and I were very pleased with the lesson. I plan to do more student led concept maps in the future.

MY NEXT STEP

As I become more proficient using the SWH approach, I am constantly re-evaluating my teaching. My next step is to continue exploring how concept maps can be used most effectively with my students and how to make them more student driven. I would like to explore the writing element of SWH. Science writing has been a challenge for my students I would like to have my students respond in writing more often to our experiments. Reflecting on how their thinking changes during a unit would also be an opportunity for science writing. I have realized that science writing may not look like other writing. It may involve more illustrating, diagramming and labeling. I will be encouraging my students to take advantage of different writing opportunities and styles.

I have enjoyed using the SWH approach and plan to continue following the approach even though my workshop training and case study work are over. I hope to help other teachers in my school district learn to use the SWH approach in their classrooms and expand on the science units that we have already begun to develop. Having seen the benefit for the students and the interest and involvement of the parents over my four years of working with the SWH approach, I truly believe that my students are more engaged and in control of their learning. I also feel more confident the science standards and benchmarks are being covered and that my students are learning more of the science concepts and making more connections.

I have begun integrating elements of the SWH approach into our health and social students units. Our dental health, five senses and community helper units have fit easily into the SWH approach. I am anxious to try others. My students have more responsibility over their own learning. I no longer just answer their questions; I teach students how to find answers on their own.

REFERENCES

Brown, M. (2002). *Arthur's animal adventure*. New York: Random House.
Harter, D. (2007). *Walking through the jungle*. New York: Barefoot Books.
Katz, L., & Chard, S. (2000). *Engaging children's minds: The project approach*. Santa Barbara, CA: Praeger.

Julie Malin
Boone Community Schools
Boone, Iowa, USA

SARA NELSON

12. SCIENCE ARGUMENTATION AND THE ARTS

INTRODUCTION

Teacher, last night at my slumber party we danced and sang our tree song!
Kindergarten Student

I could not help but smile when her teacher shared this with me. How wonderful that this student was so excited about science. It is not often that science content breaks into the world of slumber parties! However, that is the power of the Science Writing Heuristic (SWH) approach. For in addition to promoting argument-based inquiry in science, it can also be used as a springboard for the inclusion of arts-based assessments that strengthen student learning.

This particular student and her classmates collaborated with a professional musician to write and record music about what they had learned in science. Their song, titled Everybody Loves a Tree, was the result of their collaboration. By using the SWH approach to teach science, students benefit because it provides a framework for both argument-based inquiry and the inclusion of opportunities for students to share their learning in multiple formats or modes. The SWH then opens the door for music, drama, dance, and other arts to be included in the elementary science class-room.

The following paragraphs outline our experience of using lyric writing and colla-boration with a professional artist to refine and present student learning in science. It is hoped that it will encourage you to consider doing something similar in your classroom. I think that you will be amazed at what your students can accomplish while using the SWH approach and the arts.

PROJECT OVERVIEW

The past few years I have assisted elementary teachers with the implementation of the SWH in their classrooms and have thoroughly enjoyed the experience. The SWH developed by Hand and Keys (1999) is a curriculum innovation that replicates authentic science investigations by supporting students' critical thinking and problem solving strategies through dialogue, reading, and writing. Instead of the traditional laboratory format, the SWH approach asks students to articulate their research ques-tions, followed by a process of making claims and gathering evidence from investi-gations. The final component of this approach asks students to reflect upon their learning and how their ideas have changed.

B. Hand and L. Norton-Meier, (eds.), Voices from the Classroom: Elementary Teachers'
Experience with Argument–Based Inquiry, 141–149.
© *2011 Sense Publishers. All rights reserved.*

The SWH also emphasizes the use of "big ideas" or core science concepts to guide teaching and learning. For example, one first grade classroom's big idea was force is a push or a pull. Big ideas are determined by the teacher prior to the start of the unit and are often a reflection of district curriculum and/or state standards. Focusing on big ideas helps students grasp the big picture instead of just isolated facts and assists elementary teachers in laying a strong foundation for future learning in science. I like to think of big ideas as a road map for instruction. They help you determine where you would like to take your students, and help keep you headed in the right direction.

This project focused on the final reflection piece of the SWH approach and on assessing if students had captured the big idea. It came about due to a discussion with a professional musician. I had been sharing my experiences with him, and he wondered if music might fit into the approach. We started talking about how song lyrics often get stuck in your head and are remembered years later. Would the same happen if students wrote a science song? Additionally, we talked about how assessment could be more than a paper-pencil test. Would an assessment using lyric writing be able to reveal and possibly deepen student learning in science? Lastly, we wondered what impact and potential benefits might come out of a project in which students were asked to transfer science knowledge into the arts.

A project to answer these questions was designed, and we began looking for teachers that might have an interest in participating. Six elementary teachers using the SWH approach volunteered to participate (2 kindergarten, 2 second grade, and 2 fifth grade). It was decided that each class would collaborate with the musician to write and record music about what they had learned in their science units. This would be the final reflection component of their SWH units. The methods and amount of support varied, all six classrooms followed the same basic procedure that follows for writing and recording their songs.

To begin, students negotiated a list of what they had learned in small groups or as a class. What needs to be said is that science negotiations (especially your first ones) are often chaotic and may feel out of control. However, keep working on encouraging students to talk, question, and argue politely with *each other*. You may find that, as a teacher, it can be very hard to be quiet during science conversations. I recommend recording and reviewing these conversations periodically to determine how much control you have "actually" handed over to your students. Also, please remember that these conversations will probably not make it into the teaching hall of fame at least initially. They will be messy and surprising. Step in only when needed and let the students take control of the discussion.

Additional items (i.e. funny words or ideas) they wanted to include in the lyrics were also discussed at this time during science conversations. Lyric ideas were then sent to the musician for arrangement in an original song. This was followed by a rehearsal and recording time with the musician. To cap off the project, each student was given a CD to share with his/her family. This part was considered crucial, for it allowed the student to share their learning at home and created a wonderful home to school connection. The CD contained a variety of tracks such as one of the students singing their song and piano solos performed by the musician. In the following paragraphs, the process is detailed for each grade.

KINDERGARTENERS AND ONE SPAGHETTI TREE

Both kindergarten classrooms conducted a tree unit. The big idea for their units was that trees are a needed part of our lives. The teachers focused on their big idea by stressing and supporting learning situations that highlighted how trees provide or help with: (1) clean air, (2) erosion, (3) beauty, (4) food, (5) wood, (6) shade, and (7) shelter for animals. Tree units done in the past had focused on identifying tree leaves. However, after attending SWH workshops the teachers realized that leaf identification was not the big idea they wanted students to remember years later. So after much discussion, the big idea that was listed above was created. Their unit included many student activities that focused on using the SWH process. For example, students took a hike to a local park to observe trees and animal/insect life and recorded their observations in a journal. These observations, done in both pictures and words were then discussed, and questions arose from the students during the discussion. The class then worked to answer those questions using the SWH process and used their data to back up their ideas. After about four weeks and numerous questions, the teachers felt they had reached a good ending point for the unit. They were now ready to assess if students had a good grasp of the big idea and if they could present their science learning in lyric form.

One kindergarten teacher chose to start the process with a student led science talk. She started the talk by asking students to share what they had learned about trees. To help students talk to each other, and not the teacher, they were arranged in a circle on the floor with the teacher sitting outside of the circle. As they discussed, a little frog or other item was thrown around to indicate whoever's turn it was to talk. This helped cue the students as to when to talk and not to talk. During the science talk, the teacher wrote down student comments on sticky notes and then placed them on a piece of chart paper. There were a few laughs when someone mentioned something about spaghetti growing on trees as a joke! To the child's surprise and delight the teacher added this to the chart as something that might be funny to add to the lyrics. The teacher then asked students to review all of the ideas and to state whether or not they agreed with them. We were pleased to note that the final list approved by the students reflected the big idea (we need trees and the reasons that we do).

The second kindergarten teacher spilt her class into two groups. Each group had an adult to help facilitate the conversation. During the small group sharing time, students were simply asked to share what they had learned about trees. The adult wrote their answers on a piece of chart paper. The group was then asked if they agreed with the statements or not and to share why they thought the way that they did. When a conclusion of sorts had been reached both groups were brought together on the carpet. The two charts were compared. Items in common were included on a master list, and the others were debated. The teacher also chose to come up with some rhyming words that might be used in the song (e.g. air and bear) at this time. Again, this class was able to state the big idea and core concepts they had learned about trees.

When compared to their class concept maps, both classrooms reflected most, if not all, of the core science ideas taught by their teachers. Due to the age of the group, it was decided that the musician and I would finalize the lyrics. We presented a draft of the lyrics to the class for approval. They agreed with our ideas, so the

Everybody Loves A Tree!	Everybody Loves a Tree!
Music by: Eric Franzen with lyric assistance	Music by: Eric Franzen with lyric assistance
From Mrs. Johnson's Class	From Mrs. Anderson's Class-2006

C: T-R-E-E, tree – e –e –e
         Everybody loves a tree.
         Animals, you and me –e –e,
         We all need trees!
	C: T-R-E-E, tree – e –e –e
	         Everybody loves a tree.
	         Animals, you and me –e –e,
	         We all need trees!

v.1   Squirrels eat nuts and deer eat bark,
         Trees give wood for my go-cart.
         Houses, tables, paper too,
         Trees help many things we do.
	v.1 Apples, pears… coconuts,
	         trees give yummy food to us.
	         Beehives hanging in the air,
	         bees give honey for the bears!

v.2   Climbing high is scary,
         There's some yummy berries.
         No spaghetti that I can see,
         I just want a donut tree!
	v.2 Wood is used to build my house,
	         trees give wood, without a doubt.
	         Monkeys, birds and people too,
	         We live in trees, how bout that dude?!

v.3   Trees grow up and fall to the ground
         Sometimes chainsaws cut them down.
         Laying flat or standing high,
         We need trees we cannot lie!
	v.3 Trees help us in many ways,
	         this we share with you today.
	         Eating, breathing, climbing high,
	         thank a tree when you have the time!

Figure 12-1. Kindergarten lyrics.

musician went to work creating a melody to go along with the lyrics. The lyrics for each class song are displayed in Figure 12-1. As you can note, the big idea and other core ideas were present in the class lyrics.

SECOND GRADE KEEPS ON ROLLING

The second grade teachers had their classes come up with group claims about the concepts of balance and motion. Their big idea was that certain principles put items in motion or cause balance. Each group worked together to come up with a claim about balance and motion and backed it up with evidence from their experiments. During their small group conversations, many students would refer to the class concept maps and their science journals as evidence. It seemed very natural for them to use these pieces of writing to help inform their decisions. After the groups had agreed to their claims, they presented them to the class. These claims were then also discussed. Claims that were approved by the group were written down to be sent to the musician. Additionally each group added some funny parts to make the song catchy. A copy of the email that was sent to the musician is in Figure 12-2.

The second teacher chose a fairly similar path to generate lyric ideas. However, she chose to use the circle in a circle approach to assist her students in making claims. To achieve the circle in a circle approach, the teacher first divided the students into two groups. Then she had one of the groups sit in a large circle on the carpet. The second group sat inside the circle, facing their classmates. This teacher had the pairs discuss what they had learned and to make a claim backed up with evidence.

1. The bowling ball hit the Kleenex box the hardest while the marble barely pushed it at all or weight matters.

2. The little foam ball took one second to reach the bottom of the ramp as did all of the others.

3. The higher ramp made the object go faster.

4. More mass=more energy

5. Things fall at the same rate or go down the ramp at the same rate

Funny stuff: One kid yelled out this and it would be great to use it. He said warning of the bowling ball–all hands and feet to your side. Also, the class downstairs thought that it was thundering when they were rolling the bowling ball. Plus, the teacher had trouble lifting the bowling ball and it looked like she was driving a car, tipping left and right.

Fun motion words: Sliding, running, biking, jogging, climbing, walking, gliding, swinging, rolling, crab walk, sledding, slithering

Figure 12-2. Email to musician.

Motion Commotion
Lyrics by: Mrs. Penning's Class and Eric Franzen
Music by: Eric Franzen

Chorus: Motion!
        Motion!
        M-M Motion, gives a notion
        That we all can cause commotion
        M-O-T-I-O-N, Let's keep moving till the end

V1:   Different balls, race down the slide
        Fall the same so it's a tie
        WARNING! One's a bowling ball
        Hands and feet to your side

V2:   Hit the box at equal speeds
        Which has more energy?
        Listen for the biggest crash
        That's the one that has more mass

V3:   What's that thunder? Run for the door
        We're just bowling on the floor
        Lifting it with all her might
        Ms. Johnson tipped left to right

Figure 12-3. Second grade class lyrics.

Each student had their science notebook with them to refer to data that they had collected. After a short period of time, the inside circle rotated one to the left and the process started again. This activity then led into a group session in which students discussed what they had learned. They were asked to make groups claims about their balance and motion unit. These ideas were recorded on chart paper and sent to the musician.

The songs that came out of the experience were great! The lyrics for one song can be found in Figure 12-3. As you read it, note how the big idea and other core science concepts are expressed in the lyrics. This reflective activity forces students to focus on core concepts and how best to represent them. It is a wonderful reflection what the students learned in their unit.

FIFTH GRADE GOES SOUND SURFIN'

The older grades worked in small groups to write their lyrics. This then, allowed students to make claims, back them with evidence and participate in argumentation somewhat independently. They had participated in group argumentation before with their teacher, so the process was familiar to them. For these groups the teachers simply shared that they would like for them to come up with some claims and evidence about what they had learned. The students had also been studying couplets, and they wrote a few of those to include with their lyric ideas.

Sound Surfin'!

Lyrics by: Mrs. Johnson's Class and Eric Franzen
Music by: Eric Franzen

Chorus: It's sound and it's all around
It's sound and it's all around
Sound wave surfin', 'cross the town
Everywhere you turn a sound is found

V1: Sound waves make vibrations
We hear great sensations
Through all matter a sound can pass
Solids, liquids, even gas

V2: Waves vibrate from you to me
Fast ones are high frequency
Then my ear drums tell my brain
Trains and ghosts don't sound the same

V3: Strings that are short and tight
Make high sounds, outta sight
Loose and long sound real low
This is pitch I'll have you know.

Figure 12-4. Fifth grade class lyrics.

These lyric ideas were then sent to the musician over email and used in the creation of an original song, which was then emailed back to the students for review and approve. The entire writing process took approximately three weeks. The final version of one class lyrics is shown in Figure 12-4. As you can note, the big idea for the unit, all sound is made by vibrations, is represented in the lyrics.

The biggest difference between the grades we felt came at rehearsal time. The fifth graders were able to work with the musician a little more in the staging of the song. They offered ideas for sounds effects, movement, and rhythms. It was wonderful to watch the give and take between the students and the musician. Their final song was a wonderful collaboration and was highly engaging and full of energy. In fact, one student came to us the morning of recording with a whole new song that she had written the night before about sound. She had put a lot of work into the song, so the musician and I decided to record it for her. She was so excited to hear her lyrics and see her name on the CD!

REACTIONS AND BENEFITS

I wish that everyone could have been with us during the recording. The energy of the students was amazing! They knew that what they were doing was unique, and they were so focused because it was *their* song. The use of argumentation and lyric writing is not a typical approach for reflection and assessment in elementary classrooms. However, all involved were very pleased with the results, and I highly recommend the process. We were especially excited to see that all of the classrooms reflected the big idea in their songs. This adds a positive learning dimension to the project and reflects that connections between subject areas can promote deeper understandings of science concepts and impact student learning.

ENERGIZING ASSESSMENT

Having someone come into the classroom and help us create a song with what we learned in our unit titled, "We Need Trees", motivated my students to participate, and was an excellent extension activity to challenge their thinking. Kindergarten Teacher

The National Science Standards discuss how "effective teachers design many activities for group learning, not simply as an exercise but as collaboration essential to inquiry" (1996, p. 51). By collaborating to write and record music, students were offered a chance to share the depth of their learning in a way that goes far beyond a paper pencil test. There is great value in asking students to take what they have expressed in one mode (e.g. data graph) and transfer it to another mode (e.g. song lyrics). For in the process of shifting their learning from one mode to another, they are forced to focus on the critical elements of their learning. Therefore, offering them the opportunity to deepen their learning.

EXPOSURE TO THE ARTS

The current testing culture of our schools has forced many schools to shorten or in some cases abandon offering students multiple ways of expressing their learning.

Siegel (2006) shares that this practice limits students and can create a narrow and monotonous view of how student learning should be expressed. Integrated units offer students a variety of ways to express their learning in engaging and vital ways. For these units offer us the opportunity to, "envision and create curriculum that places inquiry and sign systems—art, music, dance, drama, and movement—at the center of the learning process, rather than in the peripheral position of curricular frills…" (Harste, 2000, p. 3).

MEMORY MARK

This was a great experience for the kids! … It was a very effective way for the kids to "cement" their learning of the science concepts from our motion unit.
  Second Grade Teacher

What has been even more amazing is the students' ability to retain this information years later. Below is a portion of a transcript from a second grader. She helped write the tree song in kindergarten, and this interview was done two years later.

Transcript portion of second grade student: Girl #1

R: Do you remember studying trees at all in kindergarten?

S: Yeah.

R: Ok, what do you remember about trees that you learned?

S: Well … Trees make paper.

R: Uh-huh.

S: Trees make wood for houses.

R: Uh-huh.

S: Some trees are fruit trees and then you can eat the fruit from them.

R: Yeah. How are you remembering all of those things from kindergarten?

S: Umm… well kind of that song.

R: Ok. So how does that song help you remember?

S: Well because it says a lot about a tree, about trees.

The long-term retention of concepts needs to be examined in more detail, but we found that many of the other students remembered much of the lyrics and their experiences with the musician. The fact that students could remember two years later points to the power of creating events in which meaning "is made through signs of all kinds—pictures, gestures, music—not just words" (Siegel, 2006, p. 65).

HOME TO SCHOOL CONNECTION

A copy of the lyrics (and a CD) went home with an explanation of how this correlated with our tree unit. This is excellent school-home communication and great PR. I have had parents comment on the CD and what a great idea it was. It was a way to use another medium of learning. The music mode sticks with you. Kindergarten Teacher

Using the arts to express learning in science is a great way to help learning leave the classroom. By taking the CD home students got a chance to "show off" what they had learned. We had many reports of siblings singing the songs together and playing it for grandma and grandpa.

CONCLUSION AND NEXT STEPS

Upon reflection, there were areas in which I would make a few changes to increase student learning and participation even more. For example, I would like to see the students collaborate with the musician to compose some of the music. Initially, the decision to have the musician write the music independently was chosen to assist in the management of a new project. However, now that the process is familiar, it would be good to turn over more of the composing to the students. Another area that I would like to expand on is that of possibly filming a music video that would include dance, and costumes.

The comments, smiles, and lyrics offer testimony for the use of collaboration between various professionals, and the integration of the SWH and music. If you find that you would like to give this idea a try but do not have access to an artist consider doing the following: (1) work with your school's music teacher, (2) think about doing a song to a karaoke track, or (3) consider having the students write the melody. I think that you will find that science argumentation is a great springboard for the arts in the elementary classroom.

To conclude, I would like to share some personal reflections from the musician. I share them because they offer another way of looking at this event or another form of expression.

The result was more than I expected, emphasizing to me the power of creativity and collaboration. ... As to what I observed of the students, I can not say enough. I think what they experienced was a true learning experience, and will be something they will always remember. I feel that kids, and many adults for that matter, need to be reminded of the creative power that they possess. This project really engaged the kids in that process. They created something of their own that they could feel proud of, and they will have forever. Reflection from Cooperating Musician.

REFERENCES

Hand, B., & Keys, C. (1999). Inquiry investigation. *The Science Teacher, 66*(4), 27–29.

Harste, J. C. (2000). Six points of departure. In *Beyond reading and writing: Inquiry, curriculum, and multiple ways of knowing.* Urbana, IL: National Council of Teachers of English.

National Research Council. (1996). *National science education standards.* Washington, DC: National Academy Press.

Siegel, M. (2006). Rereading the signs: Multimodal transformations in the field of literacy education. *Language Arts, 84*(1), 65–77.

Sara Nelson
Iowa State University
Ames, IA

BRIAN HAND AND LORI NORTON-MEIER

LESSONS LEARNED

Teaching in the Service of Learning

My beliefs about learning are quite different as a result of my journey. I think one can only truly understand if they've had to articulate their thoughts, wrestle with their thoughts and confidently defend them. The Science Writing Heuristic provides the framework for this to happen—both for teachers and students— and when it does, it is a powerful moment. (Written reflection from a teacher, October 25, 2008)

In reviewing the chapters put forward, we believe that there are a number of critical lessons that are to be learned. We have discussed in other settings that we believe that a guiding principle from the work of Michael Halliday (1975) is that we have to live the language as we learn about language through using language, that is, we have to experience the language of science as we use it in order to learn it. The same applies to science argument - students need to live the argument through using the argumentation process as they learn about scientific argumentation. Critically they need to be engaged in their own arguments instead of those supplied to them.

For us, this is critical to helping students transfer their understanding of science argumentation processes to future learning opportunities. We want them to be able to use these processes as scientifically literate citizens. We believe that we need to help students pose questions, explore how to tests these questions, collect data, make decisions about which data can be used to help generate a claim, produce a claim(s) supported by evidence (i.e., data plus reasoning), review what others have said about their ideas and examine how their ideas have changed as a result of the argument-based inquiry.

We believe that students need to be embedded within this complete process as part of learning about science. There is a need for them to understand this is how science, as a discipline, moves forward. There is no need for us to invent situations for students to explore – we do not have to have pretend situations where students struggle to have an attachment to the subject matter. Students are inherently interested in some of the difficult concepts of science, but rarely get to pose their own questions about these topics and thus rarely have the opportunity to negotiate meaning through a question, claims and evidence structure so that they can build an understanding that is aligned to the scientifically acceptable ideas.

All of the people involved in writing chapters for this book have used the SWH approach as a means to teaching science within their classrooms. Many of these teachers come from different school districts that have set different curriculum goals and programs for their school districts separate from any other district. The approach is about learning and not about a particular curriculum. The teachers have adapted the approach for their teaching styles and curricula. However, the science topics explored in their classrooms are framed around the "big ideas" of science as outlined by national and state science standards. These teachers are not manufacturing topics, not doing argument as a separate lesson to science, but rather building their whole science teaching around the concept of scientific argument. Students are required to negotiate science ideas publicly and privately via the many opportunities to debate questions, claims and evidence, and the relationship of these to the big ideas under study by the class.

So what are the lessons to be learned from these teachers' experiences? We believe that there are three general lessons to be learned.

1. Achieving success is not instant and easy: All of the teachers have indicated that they struggled early. This was not an easy process for them because they had to shift being in control of everything, to understanding that students are in control of their own learning. They had to separate management of the classroom from management of learning. Most often the comment we received back from the teachers is that they did not believe the students could think at "this" level. The immediate response was "why are you surprised when you have never given them the opportunity". The shift in thinking required by the participating teachers is a shift in approach – it is not a process or a strategy. Asking teachers to shift away from practices that have served them well is exceedingly difficult. The process of change is not just about asking students to be involved in argumentation processes, but it also involves teachers being part of that process. All the teachers involved in this book went through a similar learning curve in shifting their perspective of how they had/have to operate in the classroom.

The classroom environment that is required for public negotiation does require a shifting in student thinking. They have to understand that their ideas are valued and that they are expected to challenge others' ideas. Each of the teacher authors had to "give up" different things to achieve this. Some were tight on their ideas of control in the classroom and thus have had to struggle to let go. Others have a more relaxed attitude but have had to struggle with when to enter into the student conversation and when to stand back. This is the difference between a learned protocol or strategy and an approach. There are not defined steps or required procedures to follow or adhere to, but a conceptual ideal that requires us to question and challenge students' thinking if we are truly about student learning.

2. There is a need to step into the unknown: As Michelle said so nicely in her chapter – "do you want to stay close to shore or do you want to be out of sight of land". Starting something for which there is no right answer in terms of the required pedagogy is a little scary. However, we cannot be hypocrites and say you must challenge students to pose questions, generate claims and provide evidence and have confidence in their answers, if we then turn around and say to teachers here are the clear steps to achieve this. Students are trained to give back answers teachers want to hear. It is scary for them not to have each answer verified as being correct. Yes, it is scary getting started because as teachers you will struggle with being uncertain what to do with students' answers. It will be difficult shifting your questioning

patterns from confirmation to negotiating, and to do daily planning after the lesson instead of a week in advance.

As we know every student in a classroom is different and will come with different background experiences and knowledge, we also believe that every teacher will come to implementing the SWH approach with a different set of experiences and know-ledge. Thus, the adoption and adaption of the approach by any teacher is going to vary. You have focused on ensuring that they have the opportunity to discuss "big ideas of learning", focusing on questioning for negotiation, and experiencing learning science using the SWH approach.

As each teacher begins to implement the approach, we often hear the "yeah buts" that prevent them from moving forward. The barriers to their changing thinking needs to be challenged, because if we believe that students actually do construct their own knowledge, then we have to teach that way. It is a little scary but not starting is even scarier. There will be more noise in the classroom, there will be different things happening in the classroom, but students will be more engaged and talking about science and wanting to go further.

As we constantly say to all the teachers – there are no mistakes, there is only going forward. As teachers we all constantly have to improve our practice. To be accom-plished at using this argument-based approach may take several years, but you will enjoy your teaching much more than before.

3. This approach can apply to all other subject areas: As the teachers have shown in their chapters, this approach requires students to engage with language all the time. They have to negotiate orally, they have to negotiate with text when they read non-fiction text, and they have to negotiate with the text they have constructed when they write. Science is not viewed as a separate subject from language – these teachers enjoy the fact that they can create time within their language instruction to do science and vice versa. As the approach is a learning approach it is not confined to science - it is about learning anything.

While there was not lots of discussion about students using the argument structure of questions, claims and evidence in other subjects, we are constantly told by teachers how excited they are when students start negotiating with each other in mathematics using the argument structure. There is not a different learning theory being applied to each subject area. There is not a different learning theory applied to each country or culture. The context of examples, for instance, will change depending on these circumstances and factors, but the idea that learners negotiate meaning through public and private opportunities is applied everywhere. We need to under-stand that this approach is not just for science.

While there are many different nuances about implementation that have not been discussed, we have tried to provide some insight from practicing teachers to help you the reader as you implement argument-based inquiry. The teachers and professional development providers have gone through a range of different experiences as they tried to implement the SWH approach. We do not hide the fact that implementation is a challenge and there will be days when you are frustrated and want to give up. However, a fairly instant reward can be seen by simply asking your students to provide evidence whenever they make a claim. Particularly if you learn not to say anything, either right or wrong, you can no longer say, "You're nearly there". As we begin to stand back and ask students to debate with one another, the classroom environment will change. You will have to be involved in monitoring the classroom in a different way. You will have many questions about what to do next. What question would I ask? How do I plan for the next day?

Just remember, keep putting one-foot forward and the answers will come. You will mess up a few times, but in the end, it will become easier. You will go home at the end of the day mentally exhausted because you have had to listen and try to understand all the things happening in your room, particularly as you demand that students construct and critique knowledge. The next day you will return to your classroom and be excited because you now realize more students are involved more often, not just a few individuals who are seen as the "bright" students. Elizabeth Moje (2007) put forth an argument about what we need in our classrooms is the practice of socially just pedagogy.

Teaching in socially just ways and in ways that produce social justice requires the recognition that learners need access to the knowledge deemed valuable by the content domains, even as the knowledge they bring to their learning must not only be recognized but valued (p. 1).

Moje argued that the SWH approach is an example of this socially just pedagogy that she describes in the above quote. It is in the words of the teachers featured in this book that we begin to see what it means to create learning environments where all children can learn thus moving toward a truly "socially just" pedagogy.

REFERENCES

Halliday, M. A. K. (1975). *Learning how to mean*. London, UK: Arnold Press.
Moje, E. (2007). Developing socially just Subject-Matter instruction: A review of the literature on disciplinary literacy teaching. *Review of Research in Education, 31*, 1–44.

Brian Hand
Science Education
University of Iowa

Lori Norton-Meier
Literacy Education
University of Louisville

CONTRIBUTING AUTHORS

(In Alphabetical Order)

Michelle Griffen started her teaching career in a 4th – 8th grade computer lab. She has also taught 1st, 4th and 5th grades. Currently, she teaches technology and team teaches science at Riverside Elementary School in Oakland, Iowa. Since becoming the science/technology teacher she has found meaningful ways to integrate literacy, science, and technology. Michelle started using the SWH approach in her 1st grade classroom. This is Michelle's fifth year using the SWH approach. Michelle has a master's degree in science education from the University of Northern Iowa.

Brian Hand is a professor of Science Education at the University of Iowa. Brian's research focuses on two major areas. The first is on how we can use language as a learning tool to improve students' understanding of science. His work has focused on using writing as a learning tool and is now moving to focus on the use of multi-modal representation within science classrooms. This research extends the use of writing as a learning tool to include different modes of representation. The second area of research is the development of scientific argument through the use of the Science Writing Heuristic (SWH) approach. This research is aimed at helping students learn about and use science argument to construct science knowledge.

Peggy Hansen has been using the SWH approach for five years, getting the opportunity to further her love of science while learning ways to teach students using the Science Writing Heuristic approach. For twenty-four years, she has taught in the Griswold Community School District. During those years, she has taught first, second, and fifth grades. Peggy lives in Griswold with her husband, Scott, and two daughters, Britney and Brooke.

Michelle Harris has taught eleven years at Anita Elementary. During those years she has taught third, fourth, fifth, and a combination class of fifth and sixth graders. Currently she is teaching fifth grade, which includes all subject areas- science, math, reading, social studies, language arts, and spelling.

Amy Higginbotham has been interested in meeting the diverse needs of learners since she began her career as a special education teacher. She has been teaching for seventeen years. Amy currently teaches early elementary in Iowa and has had the opportunity to implement argument-based inquiry for three years.

Lynn Hockenberry is a twenty-four year teaching veteran. She implemented the Science Writing Heuristic approach in her classroom before becoming a Literacy Consultant for Green Hills Area Education Agency in Southwest Iowa. As a former teacher and now a Literacy Consultant working directly with teachers who are imple-menting the Science Writing Heuristic approach in their classrooms she has seen the power that linking science with literacy has to engage students.

Carrie Johnson's days of 'playing school' as a child led her to a career in education, spanning 18 years across kindergarten through third grade classrooms as both teacher and Instructional Strategist, and currently as Consultant for Continuous Improvement for Green Hills Area Education Agency in southwest Iowa. She has had the privilege of supporting elementary and middle school educators in their SWH classrooms the past four years. It is this group of teachers, as well as Carrie's family, friends and colleagues, who challenge and inspire her to be a better teacher every day.

Gina Johnson has engaged students in learning for ten years. During that time she has been a special education teacher, a 6th grade classroom teacher, and most recently a 3rd grade classroom teacher for the Lewis Central Community School District in Council Bluffs, IA. She holds a bachelor's degree in elementary and special education and a master's degree in curriculum and instruction. Gina is currently in her 3rd year of implementing the SWH approach. She lives in Omaha, Nebraska with her husband, Kip, and daughter, Kaylee.

Julie Malin has been teaching for twenty years. She has taught kindergarten, first and second grade. Julie is currently teaching first grade at Lincoln Elementary in Boone, Iowa.

Sara Nelson has enjoyed working with elementary students for the past 13 years. She started her career as an educator for the Science Center of Iowa and then had the opportunity to work as an elementary teacher for five years. Sara is currently a doctoral candidate in Curriculum and Instruction and has been engaged with SWH research for the past 5 years.

Lori Norton-Meier is currently an associate professor at the University of Louisville in Literacy Education. As a classroom teacher, Lori taught for seven years in an inner-city environment where many of her students lived in poverty and for whom English was a second language. This classroom experience generated many questions and she has spent recent years studying students' literate lives in and out of school contexts. Her areas of interest include early childhood literacy practices, science inquiry with embedded language practices, family literacy from a strength perspective and the role of media literacy in school curriculum.

Jill Parsons has been using the SWH approach in her 5th grade classroom for four years. It has completely changed her view of teaching and learning and her favorite part is the opportunity students have to negotiate their own meaning and under-standing. Jill graduated from Central College in Pella, Iowa, and has taught 5th grade science in the Pella Community School District for seven years.

Kari Ringgenberg-Pingel started learning with 5th graders at Harris-Lake Park Elementary in 1991. A graduate of Central College, Pella, Iowa, she decided to move back to Pella and continue to work with 5th graders in the areas of math and science. After 19 years of teaching, she can confidently "claim" that the last four years of working with the SWH has had the most profound impact on her understanding of how students learn. Need evidence for that claim? Read the book.

Cheryl Ryan has been teaching and learning with students for eleven years. During that time she has taught preschool, kindergarten, and most recently 3rd grade for the Lewis Central Community School District in Council Bluffs, IA. She holds a bachelor's degree in elementary education and a master's degree in curriculum development and instruction. Cheryl's passion for science has been greatly deepened over the past three years by the SWH approach. She lives in Council Bluffs, IA with her husband, Tom, and her four children: Nicholas, Benjamin, Allison, and Jonathan.

Julie Sander received my B.S. in Early Childhood/Special Education from Iowa State University. To fulfil her dream and passion for teaching, she taught primary grades for 5 years. During her second year of teaching, she joined the SWH research team and began implementing science inquiry investigation in the early childhood classroom. She has participated in numerous presentations on the SWH research at conferences on the state and national level. In conjunction with this research, she wrote an article titled, "Science Conversations in Young Learners", published in *Science and Children* (Sander & Nelson, Feb 2009).

Joshua Steenhoek is a fifth grade teacher at Pella Community Schools in Pella, Iowa. He graduated from Central College in 2001 with a BA in elementary education. His experience in teaching includes teaching 4th and 5th grade special education. Joshua has been teaching four years with the SWH approach.

Christine Sutherland has been using the SWH approach in her kindergarten classroom for two years. She has taught primary students in schools around the world. She is interested in providing opportunities for young students to engage in purposeful writing based on real experiences, learning and thinking. This approach has enabled her to combine creativity and inquiry to make an environment where writing in science emerges naturally.

Kim Wise is a science consultant at Green Hills Area Education Agency in Southwest Iowa. She has been providing professional development around the Science Writing Heuristic for ten years. Prior to working as a consultant, Kim was an elementary/ middle school science teacher.

CPSIA information can be obtained at www.ICGtesting.com

264885BV00005B/1/P